THE A-Z OF CURIOUS FLINTSHIRE

THE A-Z OF CURIOUS FLINTSHIRE

DAVID ROWE

For Judith
and
Ken Lloyd Gruffydd (1939–2015)
for his knowledge, humour and inspiration to aspiring local historians

First published 2015

The History Press
The Mill, Brimscombe Port
Stroud, Gloucestershire, GL5 2QG
www.thehistorypress.co.uk

British Library Cataloguing in Publication Data.
A catalogue record for this book is available from the British Library.

ISBN 978 0 7524 9328 2

Typesetting and origination by The History Press
Printed in Great Britain

Acknowledgements

BOOKS OF THIS nature would not be possible without the assistance of many people, and my grateful thanks go to the following, who have generously contributed without hesitation. However, any errors or omissions rest with no one but myself:

Abergele Field Club; Brian Taylor of Holywell & District Society; Dr Shaun Evans; the Right Hon. Lord Mostyn and the Mostyn estate; the late Mrs Nancy Hansford; the family of Jim Bentley, who did so much to record the life and times of Buckley life, and a special mention to his eldest daughter Sue, who sadly died in 2012. To Paul Davies of the Buckley Society; Tom and Iris Dillon; Chris Bailey of 'Dawnswyr Delyn'; Mick Tems of *Folkwales* online magazine; Dr Miranda Kaufmann; Peter and Johanna Kaufmann; Dale Hemphill; Roy Greaves; Mrs Louise Ankers, Head of Ysgol y Waun, Gwernaffield; Jane Forking-Russell of the Black Lion in Babell; Miss Hazel Formby; Mairi and the late Charles Wynne-Eyton; the late Major Basil Heaton; Debbie Barton and Mold Golf Club; Reverend Eirlys Gruffydd; Mike Grant of the RAF Historical Society; Len Buckley; Rhiannon Griffiths, for her uncanny knack of identifying obscure stories; the USA-based Early Television Museum; Neville Dykins; Geraint Lewis; the Venerable Bill Pritchard; Reverend Ian Foster; Reverend Paulette Gower; Rowland and Irene Tennant; Reverend Neil Kelly; Simon Gerrard; Debbie Seymour; Sylvia Jones-Davies; the Grosvenor estate; Ray Davies; Eric Keen; Colin Sheen and Bagillt History Club; John King; Jonathan Evans MP; Lyndon Jones; Lachlan Mackay; Alan Roberts; Fr John Cavanagh OFMCap; Fr Anthony Innes OFMCap; Peter Robinson; Judge Geoffrey Kilfoil; Charles Ley; Quentin Dodd; Bill Carnegie; Phil Douglas; Reverend Alan Cliff; Paul Harston of Roman Tours Ltd; Dave Healey; John Williams; Chris Bithell: Michael Owens; Peter Jones; Fr Rory Geoghegan SJ; Michael Johnson; Bernie Trickett; Jeremy Evans; Mrs Doreen Jones; Paul Buck of the British Museum; Mrs Elaine Hinks-Edwards; Mrs Gill Grunwald; Kevin Matthias; the late Dr Malcolm Seaborne; Mrs Shirley Walls; Tegwyn Thomas; Noel Barnes and Hawarden Community Council; the late Hughie Owen; Colin Barber and Rhydymwyn Valley History Society; Ian Brown and the Friends of the Froth Blowers; Viv and Eifion Williams; Clive Sparrow; Richard O. Thomas; Philip Lloyd; Mold & District Civic Society Community Archive, and the Pub History Society.

The staff of Flintshire Record Office and Mold Town Library @nswers Centre have once again provided wonderful support, and I am deeply grateful to all the personnel for their patience and considerable expertise in second-guessing my requirements. Susan Phillips for her assistance, support and helpful suggestions throughout the whole lengthy process. Paul Brighton for his reading of the draft and his helpful comments and suggestions. The editorial team at The History Press for turning the draft manuscript into the book you are reading today.

No acknowledgement page would be complete without mention of my wife, Judith, who has not only given me encouragement to tackle a third book but has proofread and provided suggestions as to the content.

My apologies to anyone I have missed; I can assure you it was not deliberate but an oversight on my part.

Diolch yn fawr

Foreword

FLINTSHIRE IS AN old county and is listed in the Domesday Book; Flint Castle features in Shakespeare, and whilst the county retained its detached portion until Clwyd came into being, the county of Caernarfon had lost the detached parts of its area to Denbighshire in the late 1920s.

Despite its age, Flintshire can, as Dr John Davies said in a lecture to the Flintshire Historical Society, be considered an overlooked part of Wales, too easy to pass through on the way westward. Its heritage is rich, whether it be historic, cultural or industrial.

The county has had distinguished historians in the last century: Sir J. Goronwy Edwards, Professor Maldwyn Jones and Professor J. Gwynn Williams, all pupils at Holywell Grammar School, are just a few examples, and still today we see others following in their footsteps.

One heartening development in recent years has been the establishment of local history societies, which have enriched our knowledge of so many parts of the county. This has been due to the enthusiasm of many individuals, and David Rowe is one of them. Although not a native of Flintshire, he has immersed himself in its history and has been especially active in the Mold area; many societies have benefited from his research.

This book, because of its nature, covers much that would be lost in longer articles but at the same time deserve mention. I am sure that it will be of interest to anyone with a love of the county and its history.

MAE SIR Y FFLINT yn hen sir ac fe'i rhestrir yn Llyfr Domesday; mae Shakespeare yn rhoi sylw i Gastell Y Fflint, a thra cadwodd y sir ei darn tir gwahanedig hyd at sefydlu Sir Clwyd, trosglwyddwyd darnau gwahanedig o Sir Gaernarfon i Sir Ddinbych yn y 1920au hwyr.

Er yn cydnabod bod Sir Y Fflint yn hen, dywedodd y Dr John Davies wrth annerch Cymdeithas Hanes y Sir ei bod yn rhan o Gymru y gellir yn hawdd ei hanwybyddu wrth deithio drwyddi tua'r gorllewin. Mae iddi dreftadaeth gyfoethog, yn hanesyddol, yn ddiwylliannol ac yn ddiwydiannol.

Magwyd haneswyr o fri yn y sir yn ystod y ganrif ddiwethaf, sef Syr J Goronwy Edwards, yr Athro Maldwyn Jones a'r Athro J Gwynn Williams, pob un wedi bod yn ddisgybl yn Ysgol Ramadeg Treffynnon. A gwelwn rai eraill yn dilyn ôl eu traed heddiw.

Un datblygiad calonogol yn y blynyddoedd diweddar yw twf cymdeithasau hanes lleol, sydd wedi cyfoethogi ein hadnabyddiaeth o lawer ran o'r sir. Mae hyn yn ganlyniad i frwdfrydedd ambell unigolyn, megis David Rowe. Er nad yw'n frodor o Sir Y Fflint, mae David wedi trwytho ei hun yn ei hanes, yn weithgar yn Yr Wyddgrug a'r cylch yn arbennig; ac mae llawer o gymdeithasau wedi elwa ar ei ymchwiliadau.

Oherwydd ei natur, mae'r llyfr hwn yn delio â llawer na châi sylw mewn ysgrifau hirach ond eto i gyd sy'n haeddu sôn amdanynt. Rydw i'n siŵr y bydd o ddiddordeb i'r sawl sy'n caru'r sir a'i hanes.

R.O. Thomas, Chairman of Council – Flintshire Historical Society
Cymdeithas Hanes Sir Y FFlint

Introduction

'If history were taught in the form of stories,
it would never be forgotten.'

THE QUOTATION, BY Rudyard Kipling, is very fitting for a compendium of local history stories dedicated to my adopted county of Flintshire. When The History Press first suggested I write the book as part of their nationwide 'A–Z' series, my first concern was whether there was enough fresh material available so that the book would not be just a retelling of previously published stories.

It would not be possible to tell tales of Flintshire without the inclusion of certain well-known places and events, but hopefully much will be new to many readers, and the more well-known tales will be viewed from a different angle. From the initial research the problem clearly became a matter of what was going to be left out, so who knows, there may be a demand for a follow-up book!

Flintshire is a county rich in heritage, sadly not always fully appreciated or promoted, and in this book I have attempted to illustrate its wide and varied history by recounting tales of people, places and events. As an incomer, and a *Sais* (Englishman) at that, I have had immense pleasure from researching the area and listening to residents' stories, but I have only scratched the surface of this fascinating county.

Throughout the centuries there have been significant changes to towns and villages in Flintshire, many of which were at the forefront of the Industrial Revolution because of their large number of mines and factories. The immigration of workers impacted greatly on many places, but the majority of communities have managed to maintain their identities throughout. The distinctive Welsh culture and language has survived all of these changes, and indeed the national identity appears to be getting stronger. One thing remains constant; the friendship and hospitality shown to incomers, like myself, who respect the uniqueness of this small nation.

There is still so much to learn about this border county and I look forward to continuing with my research. Many of the stories could justify a book of their own, but hopefully this one will enthuse the reader to look deeper into subjects that specifically interest them and share their knowledge with others. Are all the stories true, or are some 'urban myths'? Getting to the truth, or even determining facts, can be a major challenge, as often the local belief suggests a story may be true, although there is no substantive evidence to support such a claim. In this book I have written some stories I have been unable to fully substantiate, but I will leave it to you, the reader, to decide whether they are true. The following quotation by Robin Bruce Lockhart highlights the dilemma: 'The whole truth I suggest, can rarely, if ever, be written by historians either of today or tomorrow, however conscientious they may be.'

About the Author

AS WELL AS being a committee member of Mold & District Civic Society, David Rowe is a council member of Flintshire Historical Society. He has lectured extensively on a variety of local history subjects, developed and conducted a series of town trails, and provided the research for the S4C television programme related to Mold, *Y Dref Cymreig*. He lives in Mold, Flintshire, and has written two previous books on the area for The History Press, *Around Mold* and *Flintshire Pubs & Breweries*.

A

AGRICULTURE, ANIMALS AND AMPHIBIANS

The Flintshire-born writer and naturalist Thomas Pennant in his book published in 1796, *The History of Whiteford and Holywell*, describes the *pry llwyd* (badger) as 'an animal found in our parish: but neither here nor in other parts of the kingdom a common animal'. How things have changed, as it is now a common animal witnessed by the number of road signs warning of badgers. In the same book, he writes about another animal we see in great numbers: 'The sheep are numerous. They likewise are left to themselves; and become in hard weather great nuisances by their trespasses on the cultivated lands of us low-landers'.

Close the gate. (David Rowe)

The roaming of sheep across common land remains with us today and, at Moel-y-Crio on Halkyn Mountain, the gates pictured on page 13 were erected to celebrate the millennium but with the practical purpose of preventing sheep entering the bus shelter.

The winter of 2007 brought another hazard, when Flintshire County Council started to use a new type of grit made from sugar, starch and cereal, with the result that as soon as the gritter went past, large numbers of sheep converged on the road, licking off the grit. To make matters worse, they would not move to allow the passage of cars. To add to the poor motorists' frustration, on Halkyn Mountain they now have to face the hazard of toads, as can be seen from the pictured road sign, one of a few such signs within Flintshire.

Prior to the establishment of a permanent beast market in Mold, the markets were held in the High Street, but this did not meet everyone's approval, as highlighted by a report to a local newspaper in 1871:

> Mr Bellis would like to call the attention to the Board of another great nuisance, fairs particularly cattle fairs held in the main street and principal thoroughfares. These are a great nuisance to shopkeepers as side paths are full of dung and cows staring through the windows is not pleasant for shopkeepers and their customers.

Don't count them! (David Rowe)

Where is a zebra when you need one? (Jonathan Hulson)

The good people of Holywell had more to worry about than sheep or toads when, on 1 April 1859, Wombwell's Travelling Menagerie visited Holywell from Mold. It arrived at about 4 p.m. and set up in a field near Halkyn Street. The weather was not too good and the various coaches were placed in position rather hastily. The canvas that formed part of the roof was not well secured to the outer of the coaches and caravans. At about 8.30 p.m. a severe storm broke out, with heavy rain and high winds. The wind caught the underside of the canvas sheeting and turned three coaches over.

Mr Benjamin M'Bane, who had been with Wombwell's for over thirty years, had just finished his performance with his thirteen tigers. Mr M'Bane was standing on a ladder introducing the next part of his act, where he would enter a cage with five full-grown African lions, when the accident occurred. Mr M'Bane and two schoolboys, Edward Jones and David Oxford, were killed by the lions. Panic broke out amongst the audience, with people running everywhere. Houses, shops and pubs closed up and barred their doors with animals on the loose.

The three victims were buried in St Peter's cemetery with most of the town turning out for probably the largest and most elaborate funeral witnessed in the town. The band from the menagerie led the cortège and the trumpeter played a solo from *The Messiah* ('The Trumpet Shall Sound and the Dead Shall be Raised') over the graves. What happened to the lions is not recorded.

Visiting a Wombwell event appears to have been dangerous, as they had a series of 'incidents'. Near Newhaven, in 1835, a lion and tigress escaped, killing four people as well as a number of cows. In 1889, at Birmingham, an African lion escaped, and the lion and the onlooker who grabbed its tail disappeared into the city sewers, from where the lion was recaptured. Sadly the onlooker did not survive the encounter.

As well as the menagerie, Holywell boasted a circus, and this curious advert appeared in the 3 August 1895 edition of the London-published *The Era*:

> Wanted; a Good Leader, also Euphonium, to join at once. Term: Leader £2; Euphonium 32*s* 6*d*. Wire Alexandra Circus, Holywell, North Wales. NB the Leader will be required to bring a little music with him, as he will not be able to borrow the First Cornet's Books, the late leader having worn them out. Bye, bye, my gentle Austrian; sorry you forgot to take away the Cigar Box you carried your music in. Does the new suit hurt you much?

What is the story behind this, and was this an acrimonious parting of the ways?

AMERICANS AT SEALAND

For travellers entering Wales along the M56 motorway, they will see on the left-hand side the now decommissioned RAF Sealand. The runways, hangars and accommodation blocks that were located on the opposite side of the road have long since been demolished and Deeside Industrial Park now covers most of the former airfield.

The airfield dates back to the First World War, where it was the home of a variety of aeroplanes, including Sopwith Pups, Camels, and Avro 504s. In the 1920s, it also housed a packing depot and, prior to the Second World War, an aircraft storage unit was added to the site. At the outbreak of the Second World War, there was a major shortage of pilots and the base was used for flying training. Maintenance work was also carried out on Mosquitos, Lancasters and Wellington bombers.

On 15 March 1951 the United States Air Force (USAF) took over Sealand, as a satellite of USAF Burtonwood, and it became the home of the 30th Air Depot Wing. However, this was not the first that Sealand had seen of our American cousins. In St Michael's churchyard, Shotwick, can be found the grave of Lieutenant S. Morange, who was one of two American airman killed at RAF Sealand during the First World War. The body of the other airman was taken back to America for burial.

A more famous – and fortunate – renowned American aviator was Colonel Charles A. Lindbergh, who landed at Sealand on 24 November 1936. Flying in a Miles M12 Mohawk, the only one assembled and built by Phillips & Powis Aircraft Ltd at Woodhey. He was on a round-trip test flight, from Croydon to Shannon Airport, but due to fog on the return trip he landed at RAF Sealand, instead of Croydon. The RAF was requested not to publicise his arrival and, as a result, panic set in as to his whereabouts. *The Times* of 26 November 1936 carried a report stating that, due to the lack of any information, enquiries as to his whereabouts had been instituted. However, all was well in the end when he informed people where he was.

Following the takeover of the base by the USAF in 1951, the normal facilities expected by American servicemen were installed, including a ten-pin bowling alley. Rationing was still in place for locals and, with a fully stocked commissary on the base, the servicemen were naturally very popular and were regular visitors to the pubs and dance halls around the area. Certain locations were out of bounds for the enlisted men; for example, admission to the Grosvenor Hotel in Chester was restricted to officers only.

However, not everyone was happy about the presence of Americans, and on May Day the base would have to go on 'lockdown'. This was to prevent incidents between American servicemen and placard-carrying demonstrators, who were parading and chanting anti-American slogans around the perimeter. This was not a view shared by all locals, and Anglo-American relations were often fully restored by marriages between servicemen and local girls. USAF Sergeant Dale Hemphill and Audrey Henderson married in Mold, and the couple returned to Gig Harbour, Washington, on completion of Dale's posting, where they continued to live until Audrey's death in 2012.

ARTS AND ARTISTS

Flintshire is rightly proud of its cultural heritage in all fields of the arts, and in 2012 the Visual Arts Trail incorporated seventeen venues.

During the twentieth century, the county has produced many eminent and gifted artists and entertainers, and theatregoers at Clwyd Theatr Cymru will be familiar with the Emlyn Williams Theatre. Emlyn Williams (1905–1987) was born at Mostyn, Flintshire, and educated at Holywell Grammar School and Christ Church, Oxford, where he joined the Oxford University Dramatic Society. This introduction to the stage led him to a career as an actor and a renowned writer. A number of his plays reflect his childhood in a Welsh speaking, working-class family. His writing has stood the test of time, and his 1935 thriller *Night Must Fall* has had two film versions, as well as many stage revivals in both London and on Broadway, New York.

Another former Holywell Grammar School pupil, Jonathan Pryce, who also made his name in the acting profession, was born in Carmel in 1947. Following school, he attended an art college and underwent teacher training, before winning a scholarship to the Royal Academy of Dramatic Art. His fellow students included Juliet Stevenson, Alan Rickman and Kenneth Branagh. Since his early days at the Everyman Theatre, Liverpool, his career has blossomed and as well as his many television, radio and theatre successes, both here and on Broadway, he has also appeared in many films. Credits include *Tomorrow Never Dies*, *Pirates of the Caribbean* and, of course, as Peron alongside Madonna in the blockbuster *Evita*. Whilst his work has been recognised over the years with a variety of acting awards and a CBE from the Queen, he has never forgotten his roots and in the foreword he wrote for the Bagillt Heritage Society 2001 publication, *Bagillt – A Village of Verse*, he recalled the story of his father starting work at the Bettisfied Colliery, aged 14, and working chest deep in water.

Wales has always been quite rightly proud of its singers, and Flintshire has contributed to that reputation. Daniel Owen, the Mold-born author, was reputed to have had a fine tenor voice. Whilst Owen may have been known locally, he did not have the international reputation of the Trelogan-born tenor David Lloyd (1912–1969). Born into a mining family, he left school at age 14 to become an apprentice carpenter, but singing remained his first love, and he competed in local *eisteddfodau*. After graduating from the Guildhall School of Music, his career blossomed and his talent was recognised not just in the United Kingdom and across Europe, but in the United States of America. He performed in all forms of classical music, but he retained his distinctive Welsh identity and continued to perform Welsh hymns and folk songs.

Holywell boasted an operatic soprano and concert singer, Sarah Edith Wynne (1842–1897), who developed an international reputation and was affectionately known as '*Eos Cymru*', which translates into English as the 'Welsh Nightingale'.

Coming more up to date, and with certainly a different type of music, is the Coldplay lead guitarist, Jonny Buckland. Although born in London, his family moved to Pantymwyn when he was 4, and he went to the local primary school, Ysgol y Waun, before moving to the Alun School, Mold. His interest in music started at an early age and when he went to University College, London, he met the other members of what became Coldplay. Described as a 'multi-platinum and multiple Grammy-winning band', the internationally renowned group formed in 1996 and were the winners of the prestigious 'Hollywood Song Award' at the 17th Annual Hollywood Film Awards in 2013. The award was for the song 'Atlas' from the soundtrack of the film *Hunger Games: Catching Fire*, which they also performed at the ceremony.

Helfa Gelf. (Art in the Community)

The county has also been the home of very different types of artists, and it is thanks to the work of two of these that we have early views of towns which have changed almost beyond recognition and country houses that have long since disappeared or been radically refashioned.

However, we begin with an artist whose work, both portrait and landscape, is not centred on Flintshire. *The Welsh Academy Encyclopedia of Wales* describes him:

> Richard Wilson (1713–82) is the most distinguished painter Wales has ever produced and the first fully to appreciate the aesthetic possibilities of the landscape of his native country. He is considered to be the father of landscape painting in Britain and the pre-curser of Constable and Turner.

High praise indeed. Although born in Penegoes, near Machynlleth, the family moved to Mold when he was a child and, through the sponsorship of his local kinsmen – Hugh Lloyd, vicar of Mold, and Sir George Wynne of Leeswood Hall – he was apprenticed to the Covent Garden portrait painter, Thomas Wright.

Whilst living in London, Wilson gained access to the coterie surrounding Frederick, Prince of Wales. An early Wilson painting shows the Hall of the Inner Temple after a fire on 14 January 1736, and included amongst the spectators shown in the painting was the prince. Frederick was impressed by the work and Wilson was commissioned to paint a portrait of him.

Wilson was also familiar with Hogarth and enrolled in the academy set up by him around 1735. Wilson's reputation increased, and he was one of fifteen painters selected by Hogarth to produce pictures for London's newly established Foundling Hospital.

In June 1746, after Flora MacDonald was captured on Skye, she was brought to the Tower of London and Wilson painted two pictures of her; one hangs in the Edinburgh Portrait Gallery and the other in the National Portrait Gallery.

The next stage of his career is probably related to the visit to London by Canaletto, who is thought to have encouraged Wilson to visit Italy. Whilst in London, they both produced paintings of the construction of the new Westminster Bridge. Wilson had clearly amassed money from the execution of a number of lucrative commissions and embarked on a European tour from 1750, before returning to England in 1756/7. It was during this period that he was persuaded to take up landscape painting, having studied both in Venice and Rome. Whilst in Italy he gained a reputation as a landscape artist, and during his time there, he met fellow artists such as Vernet and Zuccarelli and mingled with the upper echelons of Italian society. Also during the time in Italy, his portrait was painted by Raphael Mengs (1728–1779) and it now hangs in the National Museum of Wales.

On his return to London, he was one of the thirty-four artists who founded the Royal Academy. As tastes changed, he found it more difficult to sell pictures, resulting in a major change in his finances, and as a result he became short-tempered and bitter against the world. By the mid-1770s, his appeal was in freefall and he took to the bottle and struggled with illness, whilst being in a state of poverty. In 1776, his friends found him employment as the academy's librarian,

Downing Hall. (Dr Paul Evans)

at a salary of £50 per year. He held this post until his health worsened and in 1780, at the age of 68, he returned to the home of his cousin, Catherine Jones, at Colomendy Hall. The Royal Academy, as a gesture of respect, allowed him to keep his salary, but deducted £15 in order to hire a deputy librarian.

Local legend has it that he painted the original sign for the We Three Loggerheads Inn, at Loggerheads, near Mold, as payment for his not inconsiderable bar bill. A replica of the sign can still be found in the public house today. He died at his cousin's house and his grave, marked by a Mold Civic Society plaque, can be found at the rear of Mold parish church. The final part of the inscription on his headstone roughly translates as:

> He was a benefactor to his age – he brought to it
> The beautiful teachings of Art
> And the perfect work he has left behind
> Astonishes the present age.

Wilson was a gifted, if troubled, artist whose painting legacy can be found in galleries and other locations throughout the country.

The other two artists have a direct link with the antiquarian Thomas Pennant (1726–1798) of Downing, and both were employed by him.

John Ingleby (1749–1808) was a native of Halkyn, and specialised in watercolour views. His paintings provide a unique insight, particularly into North Wales, and amongst his works are views of Caergrwle Castle, Aston Hall, Plas Mostyn, Mold town and Mold Cotton Mill. (For details of Ingleby's watercolours, refer to the National Library of Wales website, www.llgc.org.uk.) Ingleby was employed on a commission basis by Pennant and, as well as the urban views, he was also commissioned to copy coats of arms and memorials.

The other notable artist employed by the Pennant family, but on a full-time basis, was the Caernarfonshire-born artist Moses Griffith (1747–1819). Although having received little basic education and no formal art training, he nevertheless developed into a skilled draughtsman and watercolour painter. He accompanied Pennant on his various tours and his paintings and sketches covered everything from churches, country houses and general views to illustrations of birds, animals and fish, which were incorporated into Pennant's published work. We owe our understanding of long-demolished country houses to his skill, and the results of his work can be found in various establishments, including the National Library of Wales and the National Museum of Wales. Buried in Whitford churchyard, he remained a loyal servant of the Pennant family throughout his working life.

B

BANKS AND GREENFIELD VALLEY COINS

In the twenty-first century, many people have strong views on the current banking system, and the global financial crisis of 2008 did nothing to give anyone confidence in either its ethics or practices. This is not a new phenomenon, and problems have existed from the first days of coinage and, subsequently, paper currency.

The beginning of the Industrial Revolution brought new challenges, particularly as many of the factory workers on relatively low wages required payment in small denomination coins. The industrialists, recognising the need for payments to be made locally, and with insufficient coinage being produced by the Royal Mint based at the Tower of London, started issuing company tokens, such as those of Flint Lead Works.

They also established local banks, initially in Mold and Holywell, but often with mixed success as a number of these had a limited life before bankruptcy put them out of business. These banks started producing their own banknotes, and examples of nineteenth-century £1 and £5 notes issued by Mold and Holywell Banks are still in existence. As can be seen from the coin on page 24, dated 12 August 1811, a Flintshire bank was producing its own coinage, but this did not meet the needs of the growing local economy. In the late 1700s, Greenfield Valley cotton, copper and brass companies were employing in excess of 1,500 people, with weekly wages varying between 2*s* and 18*s*. With the shortage of coinage, the cotton mills started importing Mexican coins and over stamping them with the company's name; they could then be exchanged at the company's offices for Royal Mint coinage, £5 notes or larger promissory notes.

However, to Thomas Williams (the 'Copper King') of the Parys Mine Company, Anglesey, who had a factory at Greenfield, this reused coinage was not the solution. He offered to produce national coinage for the Royal Mint at his Greenfield plant without charge, providing that the copper sheets were purchased from his mills. This offer was ignored but, being a shrewd businessman, Williams was not prepared to let a business opportunity pass and at this time he was already exporting coin blanks to the Dutch East India Company in Holland.

For the home market he employed an engraver from the Royal Mint to create a Druid's head design for his coins, and hand presses were designed for the purpose. Production started in the late 1700s. On the front there was a Druid's head encircled by an oak wreath, whilst on the reverse were the initials PMC (Parys Mine Company) and the words 'We Promise to Pay the Bearer One Penny.' This not surprisingly became known as the 'Druid penny'.

Spare a copper?
(Flintshire Museum Service)

John Wilkinson, ironmaster, who was a partner with Williams in the Greenfield Copper & Brass Mills, had his own coins produced, featuring on the front a portrait of himself, which attracted much derisory comment including a poem. These were produced in one of the six factories owned by Williams in the Greenfield Valley, before the work was transferred to Birmingham. Ken Davies, in his article 'The Druid Coinage and the Greenfield Valley' published in the *Journal of the Flintshire Historical Society*, states: 'The coins struck at Greenfield set the example which was then copied throughout Britain … and set a standard which few could match. It was the standard to which the national coinage of the nineteenth century had to aspire.'

BAPTISTERY OF RHUAL AND THE EARLY CHRISTIANS

The history of the Rhual estate on the outskirts of Mold has many stories to tell, including being the site of the famous fifth-century victory of the Christian Britons over heathen invaders. Known as the 'Alleluia Victory', this is reported as having taken place at Maes Garmon and the location, adjacent to the Mold–Gwernaffield road, is marked by an obelisk, erected in 1736 by Nathaniel Griffith.

Another significant feature of the estate is located on the opposite side of the road from the obelisk. Hidden within a grove of trees in a secluded part of the Rhual parkland is a baptistery dating from the fifteenth century. After the turmoil of the English Civil Wars and subsequent Restoration of the monarchy, Rhual became a protected haven for Dissenters and their preachers, and consequently religious services were held on the estate. One important preacher, Vavasour Powell, was supported and given refuge by the owner of Rhual, Thomas Edwards (1625–1670).

Rhual Baptistery. (David Rowe)

Whilst the actual date of construction is unknown, it is believed that the baptistery, fed by a natural spring, was built at this time, and became an important base for the Dissenting cause. Thomas II (1649–1700), a former high sheriff of Flintshire, had been warned by his brother-in-law, Mytton Davies, that King Charles II was sanctioning the prosecution of Dissenters, but this did not stop Thomas from pursuing what he saw as a true religious cause.

The baptistery remains in good condition, having been refurbished in 1931 and 1991, and has been used in the recent past. It consists of a tiled rectangular well for immersions reached by a short flight of steps, a changing room (now roofless) and space for spectators, who are surrounded by an oval-shaped screen. The owner at the time of the 1931 restoration, Mrs Helena Philips, was extremely interested in the project and allowed access for the necessary work to be carried out in memory of her late husband, Lieutenant Colonel Basil Philips of the 5th Battalion (Flintshire) Royal Welch Fusiliers (RWF). The cost of the restoration and iron railings was paid for by voluntary contributions, and the granite memorial tablet was given by Mr Edward Williams, chairman of the Baptist Association. A souvenir brochure was also produced to commemorate the event. The 1991 restoration, instigated by the late Major Basil Heaton, was carried out as part of the National Eisteddfod, which was held on the estate that remains in the ownership of Thomas Edwards' descendants.

BIBLES – COMMEMORATION AND MINIATURE

Although it is impossible to obtain exact figures, there is little doubt that the Bible is the world's bestselling and most widely distributed book. A survey by the Bible Society concluded that around 2.5 billion copies were printed between 1815 and 1975, but more recent estimates put the number at more than 5 billion. By the end of 1995, combined global sales of *Today's English Version (Good News) New Testament and Bible* (copyright for which is held by the Bible Societies) exceeded 17.75 million copies, and the whole Bible had been translated into 349 languages; 2,123 languages have at least one book of the Bible in that language.

In previous centuries, it is likely that this was the only printed book a family would possess, and these were often used to maintain a family tree or record notable events such as births, marriages and deaths. Bibles were sometimes also given as gifts if people were undertaking long journeys, or in the case of our first subject, going off to fight in a war.

Henry Darbyshire was the youngest son of Richard Darbyshire, the teetotal landlord of the Glynne Arms in Hawarden. He was permitted to suspend the

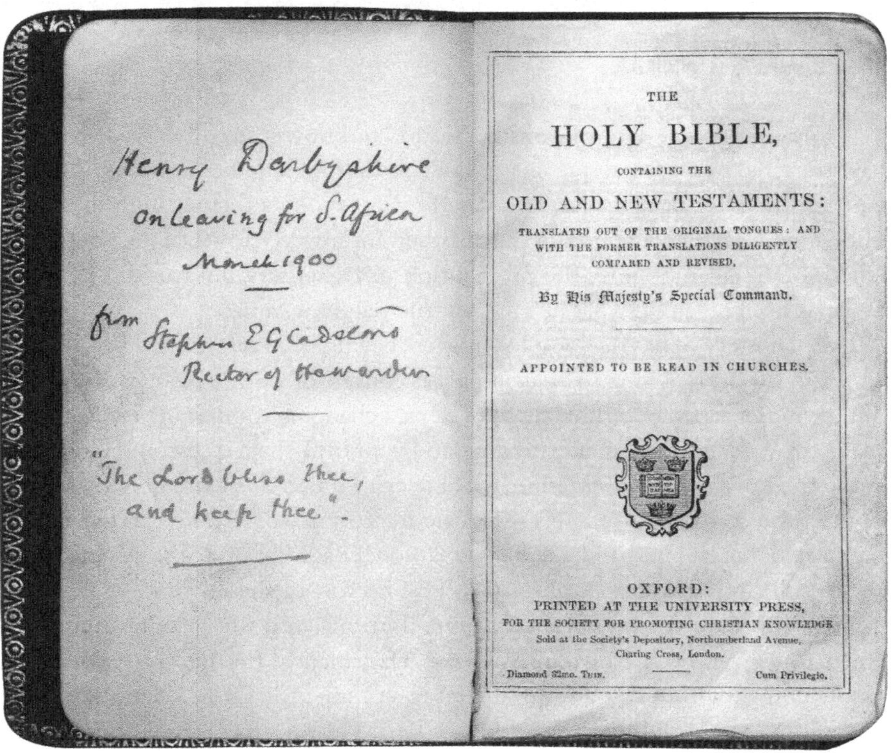

Henry Darbyshire
on leaving for S. Africa
March 1900

from Stephen E G Gladstone
Rector of Hawarden

"The Lord bless thee,
and keep thee".

THE
HOLY BIBLE,
CONTAINING THE
OLD AND NEW TESTAMENTS:
TRANSLATED OUT OF THE ORIGINAL TONGUES: AND
WITH THE FORMER TRANSLATIONS DILIGENTLY
COMPARED AND REVISED.

By His Majesty's Special Command.

APPOINTED TO BE READ IN CHURCHES.

OXFORD:
PRINTED AT THE UNIVERSITY PRESS,
FOR THE SOCIETY FOR PROMOTING CHRISTIAN KNOWLEDGE
Sold at the Society's Depository, Northumberland Avenue,
Charing Cross, London.

Diamond 32mo. Thin. Cum Privilegio.

Boer War Bible. (Susan Phillips)

Need to go to Specsavers.
(Rhiannon Griffiths)

last year of his apprenticeship at Sandycroft Foundry, Deeside. An accomplished horseman, he enlisted in the Imperial Yeomanry Cavalry in 1900, to fight in the Boer War. Prior to his departure, he was presented with the pictured bible (on page 26) by the rector of Hawarden, Reverend Stephen Edward Gladstone, the second son of the eminent Victorian prime minister, William Ewart Gladstone. It is believed that Bibles were presented to all the Hawarden men who took part in the Boer War, but sadly six of them serving with the 2nd Battalion RWF, including George Frederick Fox and Charles Richard Alfred Toller, did not return. The dead are commemorated by a memorial plaque in St Deiniol's churchyard, Hawarden.

Henry survived the war, and on his return he was presented with a watch, purchased through public subscription, by Lady Cavendish at the front of the Glynne Arms. The watch and Bible remain in the possession of the family, and we will hear more of Henry later in the book.

Bibles come in all shapes and sizes, but none are quite as small as the above owned by Miss Rhiannon Griffiths of Mold. The leather-bound, chained Bible was found by her father in a box of discarded rubbish. It is one and five-eighths inches long and one and one-sixth of an inch wide, so a magnifying glass is required to read the tiny print. On the base of the lectern is the following inscription:

Chaining of Single Books in Churches

The chaining of single books in churches originated in the injunctions given by Edward VI to the '*Clergie and Laitie*' in 1547 and printed in Grafton in which they ordered 'to provide within three *moneths* next after *visitacion* one *boke* of the whole Bible of the largest volume in English, and within one twelve *moneth* after the *saied visitacion*, the *Paraphrasis* of Erasmus the same to be *sette uppe* in some convenient place within the churches.' This injunction was repeated by Elizabeth I, in 1559. Whilst the actual origin of this practice is unknown, it is believed to have originated in medieval times. Various arguments have been put forward as to its purpose, but it seems very probable that the Churchwardens would, for their own sake, adopt that method of protecting the church's property.

BOXING – 'BOYO' GREAVES

Not so many years ago, amateur boxing was considered a rite of passage and character-builder for many boys and young men. Its popularity crossed all classes of society, and it was often the premier sport in many public schools and the armed forces. Boxing remains a significant sport in the internal and inter-service competition between the various branches of the forces. Although, in these days of health and safety consciousness the forces, along with local amateur clubs, are now required to carry out detailed risk assessments.

Open-air boxing with a dog hazard. (Royston Greaves)

Changes in attitude towards this old sport, and improved medical advice, have resulted in many local clubs closing and the number of boxing clubs has considerably decreased. Boxing tournaments were a popular spectator sport and were held both indoors and, more surprisingly, outdoors. Pictured is one outdoor tournament, held in June 1946 at the Mold Recreation Ground.

In August of the same year, as part of the Mold Urban (Welcome Home to the Forces) Central Fund and Local Charities, a carnival boxing tournament was promoted by Gerry Greaves, in association with the Army Cadet Force, at the Drill Hall in Mold. Gerry Greaves, off Flint, was better known locally and nationally by his ring name, 'Boyo'. He started his professional career in 1938, at the young age of 17, and continued boxing until 1947. In 1938 he enlisted in the Royal Navy, where the sport was encouraged and, whilst serving aboard the transport ship HMS *Dalhousie* in India, he fought and beat on points Hara Pasha, welterweight champion of India.

During his professional career he won over forty bouts, but unlike today, the rewards were not great and, on 26 October 1938, for beating Jackie Jones, of Star Crossing on points, he received the grand sum of 12*s* 6*d*. Mind you, according to the letter from the promoter Lionel Summerton, he was to receive the same amount, win, lose or draw! Amongst his many opponents was Freddie Mills, the world light heavyweight champion from 1948 to 1950.

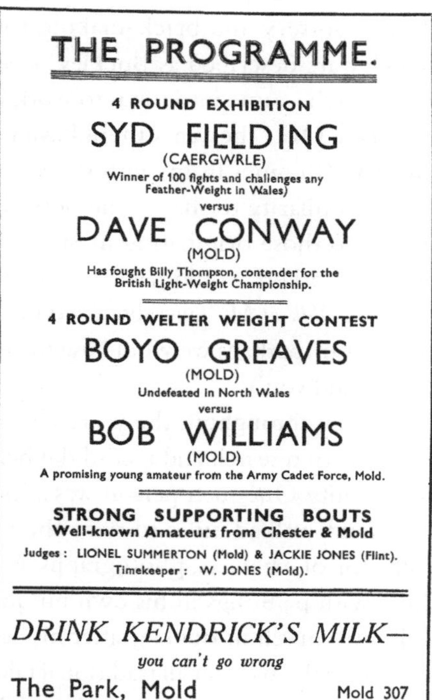
THE PROGRAMME.
4 ROUND EXHIBITION
SYD FIELDING
(CAERGWRLE)
Winner of 100 fights and challenges any Feather-Weight in Wales)
versus
DAVE CONWAY
(MOLD)
Has fought Billy Thompson, contender for the British Light-Weight Championship.
4 ROUND WELTER WEIGHT CONTEST
BOYO GREAVES
(MOLD)
Undefeated in North Wales
versus
BOB WILLIAMS
(MOLD)
A promising young amateur from the Army Cadet Force, Mold.
STRONG SUPPORTING BOUTS
Well-known Amateurs from Chester & Mold
Judges: LIONEL SUMMERTON (Mold) & JACKIE JONES (Flint).
Timekeeper: W. JONES (Mold).
DRINK KENDRICK'S MILK—
you can't go wrong
The Park, Mold Mold 307

Carnival boxing programme. (Royston Greaves)

To prove nicknames are not a new phenomenon, other opponents had such wonderful names as 'Nipper' Bennett, 'Butcher' Jones, 'Babe' Risko, 'Kid' Tanner, 'Dixie Kid' and 'Tipton Slasher'! The last one is not to be confused with a nineteenth-century prizefighter called William Perry from Tipton, who had previously used this name. Following his retirement from the ring, Gerry trained local lads, opened a gym in Denbigh Road, Mold, and for a number of years he served as the Welsh national amateur coach. In 1999, his services to sport within the local community were recognised and he was given an award by the Flintshire Sports Council.

BUCKLEY MON

Sadly, one of the casualties of our more mobile society and television 'speak' is our dialects and colloquial expressions. A sociological survey carried out a number of years ago in Glasgow found many 'cockney-ed' pronunciations, and this was put down to the influence of television programmes such as *EastEnders*.

As a child growing up on Tyneside, the author could once identify differences in the spoken word between areas as little as a mile apart. Flintshire was no different, with people originating from Flint being described as '*off*' Flint, and the dialect on Deeside described as 'Squelch' – a mixture of Welsh and Scouse!

The most unique dialect, and sadly almost dead, is that previously used in the former pottery and brick-making town of Buckley. Those originating from Buckley are described as Buckley '*mon*', reflecting the speech influences of the workers who came into town to work in the extensive collieries, brickworks and potteries. Over the years there have been considerable arguments as to where this dialect comes from, with the weight of public opinion being that it bears a great similarity to that of the potteries. Certainly many of the words are very similar to those originating in Stoke and district, and it does seem logical that pottery workers would have migrated to Buckley. The late Dennis Griffiths in his book *Talk of My Town* discussed many of these sayings, and for the uninitiated amongst us, perhaps we would use the expression 'I conna meke thee oot' ('I can't understand you').

Buckley, throughout the years, has been fortunate to be gifted with *mon* who continue to research and record the heritage and social history of their town and community. One such person was a local chemist, the late Jim Bentley, who not only field-walked miles to trace the town's industrial past, but was also a great collector of artefacts, photographs and local folk tales. He illustrated many of these with paintings in his own unique style, several of which were donated to St John's church in Buckley after his death.

Among the wonderful traditional tales he recorded in pictures and words is that of the 'Hangman that Hanged Himself.' It relates to a hangman who used to travel

The hangman who hanged himself! (Bentley family)

Bill 'Warrior' Roberts, RWF.
(Iris Dillon)

between Chester Assizes and Ruthin Assizes via Buckley Mountain, and tradition has it that he used to stay overnight at the Duke of York public house in Buckley. Locals, being what they are, quizzed him as to his business but, not wishing to advertise the fact that he was a public hangman, he always avoided answering. However, on his last visit he accidentally revealed his profession, whereupon the astounded locals persuaded him to demonstrate his technique. This he did by standing on the table, fastening the end of the rope to a beam and placing the noose around his neck. A local tipped up the table, hence the 'hangman who hanged himself'. This particular story is attributed to a number of places across the United Kingdom, but none will have been as well-illustrated as that by the Buckley *mon*.

The Buckley Jubilee was first established in the nineteenth century and continues to be celebrated, as an annual event, into the twenty-first century. Led by the Royal Buckley Town Band, residents parade from the Common, but during the First World War many Buckley *mon* were away serving in France with the Royal Welch Fusiliers. One such *mon* was the bandmaster Bill 'Warrior' Roberts (pictured on page 31) who, whilst he had his own band in Buckley, also played in a number of others, including the Royal Town Band, Bob Smallwood's Band and Buckley Old Tyme Band.

After a spell on the front line the unit, with the Buckley lads, moved back to a rest camp for rest and recuperation. The late Herbert Bellis, in an article in *The Common Interest*, detailed what happened next:

> One afternoon my uncle, Bill Roberts, took out his cornet and started to play as he marched through the line of tents. On his return journey a crowd of Buckley lads called out to him. 'Is the sun affecting thee Bill?' He replied, 'Don't you lot know what day it is? We are just going around the Cross, it's Buckley Jubilee day'. Many a tear was shed as the other lads joined in, and followed my uncle, with the cornet, and so took part in the Jubilee even if it was in France.

How Bill got the nickname 'warrior' remains a mystery, and some of the explanations put forward would no doubt leave the author open to libel charges.

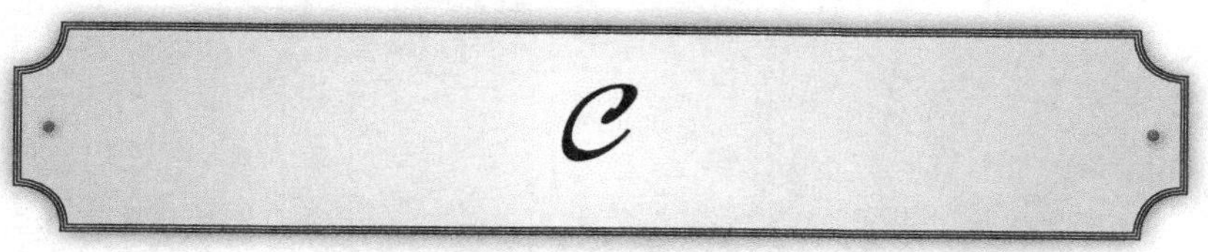

CHURCHES

The county contains many fine churches, some of whose origins go back to medieval times, and these buildings are worthy of a book dedicated just to their stories.

One significant period in church building occurred after the 1485 defeat of Richard III at the Battle of Bosworth, by Henry Tudor (Henry VII). The mother of Henry VII was none other than Margaret Beaufort, Countess of Richmond and Derby, and she is credited with the rebuilding of many churches, including those at Holywell, Northop and Mold.

However, pre-dating these particular churches is St Mary's parish church, Cilcain. Situated in the centre of the small village, there has been a church on the site since Norman times and the current church contains features dating from the fourteenth, fifteenth and sixteenth centuries. These include decorative wrought-iron gates by the Davies brothers of Bersham. Originally commissioned by Sir George Wynne of Leeswood Hall, these gates, complete with the Wynne heraldic symbol of a dolphin, were originally installed in St Mary's parish church, Mold. They were commissioned at the same time as the magnificent white gates at Leeswood Hall and the black gates now at the entrance to Tower, a fifteenth-century castellated house near Nercwys. Gwysaney Hall, on the outskirts of Mold, has a garden screen of three gates also produced by the brothers for Mold parish church.

Without doubt, the major treasure of the Cilcain church is the medieval carved wooden nave roof. This magnificent structure has carvings of figures, flowers, animals, faces and, added at a later date, the coat of arms and monogram of the Buddicom family of Penbedw. There is a mystery related to the origin of this roof – its size indicates that it was made for a much larger building. Various suggestions have been put forward as to which building the roof came from, with the most popular being that following the dissolution of the monasteries, it was brought from Basingwerk Abbey at Greenfield. From surveys of the buildings at Basingwerk, it does not appear that the roof would fit any of the buildings on that site. If this is indeed the case, where did the roof come from? A mystery that still needs to be solved.

The mystery roof. (David Allen)

The second church could not be more different than that of St Mary's at Cilcain. Situated in the parish of Hawarden, this church is one of the many hidden gems of Flintshire. The church of St John the Baptist, Penymynydd, was built of local stone at a cost of £3,000, the bulk of which, financed by Sir Stephen Glynne of Hawarden Castle. The architect was a talented artist, the London-based John Buckler, who was also responsible for the design of Halkyn Castle for the Grosvenor family. The church was consecrated in 1843, and the priest in charge from this date until 1864 was the Reverend John Ellis Troughton; it is his efforts in its enrichment that make it quite unique. Details of his work covers four pages of the 'Imaging the Bible in Wales' website, and the book *Biblical Art in Wales* includes the following extract from the Ecclesiological Society journal, *The Ecclesiologist*, on his work:

> Today we are about to introduce our readers to a monument of clerical art so remarkable, that we almost regret that its distance from London (lying as it does just within Wales) must always be an obstacle to the influence which its example might otherwise carry. Every window is filled with painted glass, designed and burnt by himself [Mr Troughton], comprising subjects on grisaille grounds, of very creditable execution.

High praise indeed, but Troughton's work during his ministry at Penymynydd was not confined purely to stained-glass windows. During his twenty-year incumbency he also completely transformed the interior, which includes paintings, mouldings and reredos around the altar. His work covers much of the surface of the church. The oil paintings are stencilled copies of pictures by the German artist Friedrich Overbeck (1789–1869), whilst other elements of the work owe much to the advice he received from an archaeologist and architect friend, the Yorkshire-born R.P. Pullan (1825–1888).

In 1898, W.E. Gladstone was so impressed with his work that a memorial tablet with the following inscription was erected in the church: 'He used his rare gifts of genius and taste in himself adorning all the interior of this church by colouring, frescoes, sculptures and window staining. With much labour, but no detriment to the faithful discharge of his manifold Parish duties.'

In addition to his parish duties, he remained an active member of the Hawarden Literary Society. In 1861 Troughton, along with another 1,500 people, is recorded as having attended the annual festival of the Hawarden Literary Scientific Institution near the ruins of the old medieval Hawarden Castle. In 1864, he was appointed rector of Aberhafesp, Montgomeryshire, although by then his extensive enrichment of St John the Baptist church could be considered complete.

The church remains a very active place of worship, and in addition has a monthly open day when members of the public, including travellers from faraway London, are welcome to view the remarkable work of a former curate.

At the other end of the county will be found All Saints' church at Ffynnongroyw. The architect of this was the renowned Victorian George Edmund Street, whose other works include the Royal Courts of Justice in London, the American Cathedral in Paris and the Crimean Memorial church in Istanbul.

The work of the gifted priest. (Eric Keen)

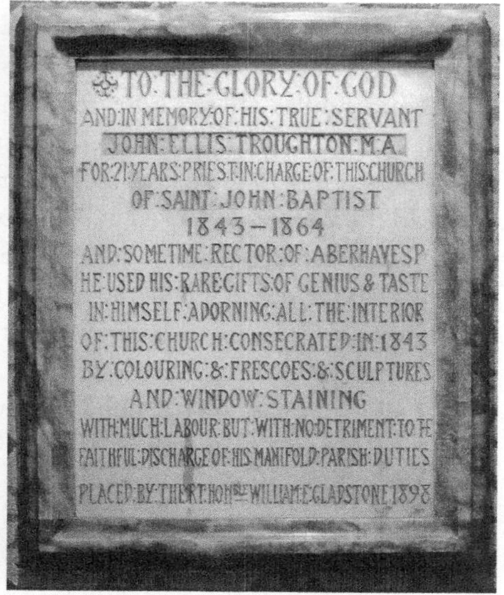

Memorial tablet. (Eric Keen)

Most churches have bells to summon the faithful to prayer, but St James parish church, Holywell, had a unique method of calling its worshippers to services and it was known as '*Gloch Bach*' (Small Bell). The church, rebuilt in the mid-eighteenth century, is situated on the side of a steep hill, which prevented the bells being heard in the town above. Consequently the Gloch Bach was slung from the shoulders of a man known as the 'walking steeple', whose knees, protected with padding, knocked against the bell to ring it as he walked around the town to summon people to church. This method lasted until the middle of the nineteenth century.

CROSSES

Stone crosses, many dating from the early medieval period, were once commonplace throughout the county, but during the sixteenth century they were often considered idolatrous. In 1561, Bishop Davies of St Asaph issued the following decree: 'That every of them [clergy] shall forthwith *avoyd*, remove and put *awey*, or cause to be put away, all and every *moniment*, *syne* and token of all and every *fayned* religious and other *superstyiyons* …' No specific mention of crosses, but this was not the case in a 1643 Act: 'Monuments of Superstition of Idolatry to be demolished … All crosses in, or upon all and every of the said churches … to be taken away and defaced.' As a result, many of these crosses were defaced or destroyed, although traces can still be found.

In the 1886 publication *Old Stone Crosses of the Vale of Clwyd*, a number of these are listed: Cilcen, Cwm, Flint, Halkyn, Newmarket (now Trelawnyd), Llanasa, Whitford and Ysceifiog. One factor that is fairly common is that the bases of many crosses have grooves caused by the sharpening of arrowheads, pikes, swords, knives and similar objects. Our forefathers also appear to have wished to be buried in the shadow of the churchyard cross, and there were often many graves in close proximity to the location of the cross. In some cases, individual wills even specified the wish to be buried in the proximity to the cross.

The most complete churchyard cross can be found at St Michael & All Angels church, Trelawnyd, and is believed to date from the twelfth century. Standing over 11ft high, it pre-dates any church on the site and therefore it is believed that it was used by itinerant priests.

Not all crosses are to be found in churchyards, and *An Inventory of Ancient Monuments* lists one such cross at Maes-y-Groes on the Llanferres–Cilcain road:

> A House of 2 stories, with mullioned windows; apparently of the early century, with some older buildings. On an inner gatepost is a deeply incised Latin cross; at the bottom of the same post is a device evidently intended as a heraldic shield with an inescutcheon. Between the cross and the shield is the date 1795.

The post is described as being 4ft 8in high, 1ft broad at the base, and 8in thick, made of limestone. The purpose of this has not been identified, but local tradition is that it was the point where the army led by St Germanus, travelling to the Alleluia Battle, crossed the field. If this is not the explanation, then why would someone place such an item in this location?

Maes-y-Groes Cross. (David Rowe)

Without doubt the most significant cross in Flintshire that is not located in a churchyard will be found in a field some 1.5 miles from the village of Whitford, and called Maen Achwynfan (also called Maen Chwyfan). The free-standing 'wheel cross' is claimed to be the tallest in Britain. Thomas Pennant, in his *The History of the Parishes of Whiteford, and Holywell*, describes it as follows:

> This is an elegant form and sculpture; is twelve feet high, two feet four inches broad at the bottom, and ten inches thick. The base is let into another stone. The top is round, and includes, in raised work the form of a Greek Cross. Beneath, about the middle is another, in the form of St Andrew's: and under that, a naked figure, with a spear in his hand. Close to that, on the side of the column, is represented some animal. The rest is covered with very beautiful fret-work, like what may be seen on other pillars, of ancient date, in several parts of Great Britain …

The cross is thought to date from between the tenth and eleventh centuries and Rowland Tennant, in his book *A History of Six Villages*, describes the carvings as having similarities to those of both 'Celtic and Viking workmanship, having Celtic crosses, chains, knot work and animals'. Once again its origin has not been proven, so its purpose and makers remain a mystery.

COCKPITS AND THE TWO FAT HENS

The practice of cockfighting was made illegal in England and Wales by the 1835 Cruelty to Animals Act, although it is believed to be still carried out in some areas, as well as remaining a legal activity in a number of other countries. The cockpit pictured overleaf can be found in the St Fagan's Natural History Museum, Cardiff, and this seventeenth-century circular thatched cockpit stood originally in the yard of the Hawk & Buckle Inn, Denbigh. However, it is typical of the type of pit building often attached to public houses. A lease dated 16 February 1749 between

Cockpit. (Dave Healey)

Thomas Eyton of Leeswood Hall and George Berks of Mold, Gent., details one particular building in Wrexham Street, Mold: 'messuage, stables, cockpit and garden in the town of Mold called the Red Lyon. The Rent for this property is £10 and 2 fat hens in January and 2 days reaping at harvest time.' No doubt the amount of rent can only make today's licensee green with envy.

CUSTOMS AND TRADITIONS

Customs and traditions were once commonplace throughout towns and villages and whilst we are happy to see the back of some, such as cockfighting, the passing of others into obscurity is often tinged with a touch of sadness, and perhaps an onrush of nostalgia. However, the Welsh carefully guard some of these traditions, and we have to thank the enthusiastic volunteers of these folk groups who work to keep them going. Amongst the bodies operating in Flintshire is the Welsh folk dance group, Dawnswyr Delyn, who continue to make the following available to the public.

The first is the 'Cadi Ha', and this is believed to have been started by miners from Bettisfield Colliery in Bagillt. This is a form of morris dance that existed in the coal communities of Flintshire from as early as 1815. It is for eight dancers plus two comic characters, Bili the Fool and the Cadi, a man dressed up as a woman. It is traditionally danced in the month of May, and comprises a double-stepped hanky-waving start/stop processional. The Cadi Ha is named after the *Cadi*, or 'Kate', and the *Ha* is from the Welsh word for summer. The branch bearer is a character not commonly found in other morris dances, and he is the only person not 'blacked up'. He carries a branch of gorse in flower. During the dance, a song is sung in Welsh, with about as much depth of meaning as most morris songs, and the Reverend Eirlys Gruffydd has kindly translated one version of the song:

THE CADI HA (Translation: *Cadi* = an effeminate male)

Hwp Ha Wen, Cadi Ha	Push the white summer, Cadi
Morys stowt	fat Morris
Am yr uchla neidio	see who can jump highest
Fy ladal i a'i ladal o,	my ladle and his ladle
A'r ladal ges i genthyg	and the ladle that I borrowed,
Cynffon buwch a chynffon llo	the cow's tail and the calf's tail
A chynffon Rhisiart Parri'r go	and Richard Parry the blacksmith's tail
Hwp dene fo	push that's it.
A fi di gŵr y rhuban coch	I'm the man with the red ribbon
Neidiaf dros y fanfa,	I'll jump over the stile
Hwp dene for!	*Etc.*

The Cadi Ha. (Eric Keen)

Mari or 'Shergar'? (Mick Tems)

The tradition continues in Holywell town centre, where children from Flintshire schools take part in the Gwyl Cadi Ha Festival, which is normally held on the first Saturday in May.

The second custom originated in South Wales, and was used to mark the passing of the darkest days of midwinter, so it coincides with Christmas and New Year celebrations. The tradition involves the arrival of a horse's skull decorated with ribbons, and its party, originally dressed up as Sergeant, Merryman, Punch & Judy, at the door of a house or pub, where they sing several introductory verses. Then comes a battle of wits in which people inside the door and the *Mari* party outside, exchange challenges and insults in rhyme. At the end of the battle, which can be as long as the creativity of the two parties holds out, the Mari party enters with another song.

The late Geoff Jenkins and Chris Bailey of Dawnswyr Delyn observed this custom and, about twenty years ago, decided to introduce the custom to Flintshire. It was necessary to obtain a horse's skull, and Chris contacted Clutton's abattoir in Marchwiel, who let them have the skull of a racing horse. This was apparently just after 'Shergar' went missing, but they would not give them the name of the animal. The skull was wired and a system created to enable the jaw to open and close. The Flintshire Mari, nicknamed 'Shergar', has been used to entertain many people and as a consequence has raised thousands of pounds for charity. So next time you see a horse's skull bedecked in ribbons and, accompanied by some strangely dressed people, make sure you follow it to local hostelries.

Not so correct (and whether it is still followed we will leave up to the reader to decide) is a practice called 'bundling'. This was a practice prevalent throughout Wales, where it was said that courtships were carried out in bed. Described in the infamous 'Blue Books', *The 1847 Report on Education in Wales* as 'Incontinence', initially bundling involved both parties being wrapped in blankets, or sacks, and being able to spend time or even the night together without any improper behaviour taking place. However, clearly this was not acceptable to some sections of society as such barriers could be removed quite easily. The Reverend William Jones, vicar of Nevin, had this to say on the subject:

> Want of chastity is flagrant. This vice is not confined to the poor. In England, farmers' daughters are respectable; in Wales they are in the constant habit of being courted in bed. In the case of domestic servants the vice is universal. I have had the greatest difficulty in keeping my own servants from practising it. It became necessary to secure their chamber windows with bars to prevent them from admitting men. I am told by my parishioners that unless I allow the practice I shall very soon have no servants at all, and that it will be impossible to get any.

CYCLING

We still often hear complaints about cyclists, particularly if they happen to be on pavements. Well, this is not a new phenomenon, and riding on pavements was not restricted to children, as reported in the *Cheshire Observer* on 7 July 1887, when magistrates took a dim view of such antisocial behaviour. James Henry Atkin, a schoolmaster of Shotton, appeared before Birkenhead County Magistrates' Court for riding his tricycle on the footpath at Eastham, and was fined 2*s* 6*d* and costs. He was warned to be more careful in future and left the court with the following words ringing in his ear: 'You pay no rates, no duty nor anything else, and yet you take the whole pavement to yourself. These tricycles and bicycles are the greatest nuisance in the world.'

Trike me home. (Ray Davies)

According to a report of Caergwrle Petty Sessions in the *Cheshire Observer* of 9 February 1895, John McLennan Jones, colliery clerk of Pontybodkin, was summoned by Robert Lloyd, inspector of main roads under Flintshire County Council, for riding a bicycle on the footpath near the Hartsheath Lodge. The defendant admitted the offence, and was fined 10*s* and costs.

What would those magistrates make of today's traffic?

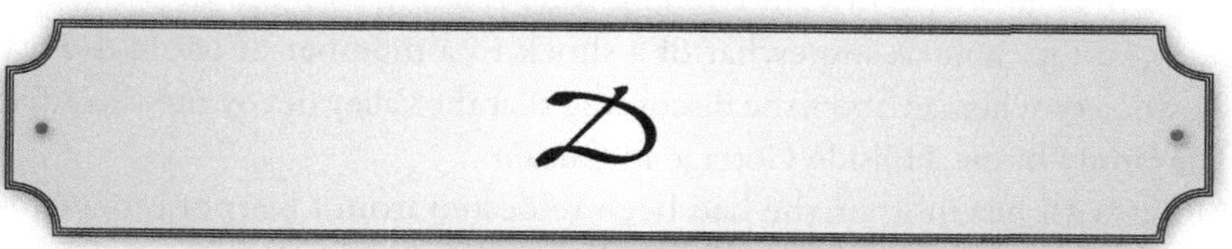

DECOY SITES, A THATCHED COTTAGE AND CORSETS

Prior to the outbreak of the Second World War there was great concern that the Luftwaffe would bomb airfields and factories, so consideration was given to defending such installations by means of decoy sites. Under the command of Colonel John Fisher Turner a number of different types of sites were established.

Daytime 'K' sites consisted of dummy aircraft, the mowing of fields to represent runways and perimeter tracks, and ploughing to represent bunkers and buildings. 'Q', or night decoy sites, consisted of various lamps which mimicked the lights of an operational airfield, and 'QF' night decoy sites used various forms of fires to deceive enemy bombers, and these were used for a variety of installations. The RAF airfields at Sealand and Hawarden, along with the aircraft factory at Broughton and Shotton Steelworks, all had decoy sites.

Safe haven, or possible target? (Nancy Hansford)

In 1941, the decision was made to provide a QF site at Cilcain to cover the Valley Works at Rhydymwyn. The key issue relating to these sites was that of secrecy, and it came as somewhat of a shock to a member of Mold & District Civic Society when, in 2006, she discovered that the Valley decoy site was adjacent to her family home, Hillside Cottage in Cilcain.

Along with her mother, she had been relocated from Liverpool to avoid the bombing of the city, but little did she know the danger she was in. A speaker giving a presentation to the Civic Society informed the audience, and a shocked Nancy Hansford, that their picturesque thatched cottage could well have been a target of the regular bombing raids. As an aside, Nancy's mother believed that no matter the circumstances, ladies should always be properly dressed. In her case, at the first indication of a bombing raid, even if in the middle of the night, she insisted on getting dressed, complete with corset!

DOCTOR LIVINGSTONE AND THE FLINTSHIRE SCHOOL MONITOR

The famous words 'Dr Livingstone, I presume?' were spoken by Henry Morton Stanley when he first met David Livingstone in a remote African village. Stanley was an illegitimate child, from Denbigh, whose name at birth was John Rowlands. Long before achieving national fame, he had a connection with Flintshire. He was a monitor (stand-in teacher) at the National School at Brynford, Holywell, and then went from there to a similar capacity at the National School, King Street, Mold, where a plaque in the now-demolished school commemorated the event. Even after that historic meeting with Dr Livingstone, his historic links with the area were not forgotten. In August 1873, J. Overy, a clothier and outfitter of Foregate Street, Chester, ran an advert in local newspapers. This took the form of a telegram purporting to come from Livingstone, and commenting on the clothes brought by Stanley from the said firm. What would today's trading standards make of this bogus claim?

DOMESDAY AND THE CENSUS RETURN OF 1891

Flintshire at the time of the production of the Domesday Book in 1086 was very different from the county we know today. It stretched from the River Clwyd to the edges of Chester, and included a detached portion, Maelor Saesneg. This former detached portion included the villages of Bangor-on-Dee, Bettisfield, Bronington, Hanmer, Penley, Tybroughton, Willington and Worthenbury. Excluding this portion, the total population was 293, listed by the various classes of men, knights, burgesses, villeins, ox men, bordars, serfs etc. However, as Domesday generally only covered the head of the household, it has been calculated that on average there were five people in each household, giving an overall minimum population of around 1,200.

This is virtually a quarter of the recorded population of Flint town in 1891, so clearly the area at the time of Domesday was not heavily populated. Due to the various county boundary changes that have taken place over the intervening years, it is difficult to draw direct comparisons, so caution needs to be exercised when comparing data from different census returns.

We take for granted our right to vote, even though many people choose not to exercise this hard-won right, but in 1888 only approximately 24 per cent of the population were included on the Flintshire electoral registers. At this time, two thirds of the population were Welsh-speaking, with approximately one quarter of residents unable to speak English, but in the 1971 census less than 1 per cent were Welsh-speaking only.

The two main occupations for males listed in the 1891 census were firstly mining and quarrying and secondly agriculture; whilst for females, over half were employed in domestic service. Overall employment levels fluctuated, but in 1891, 83.4 per cent of males and 27 per cent of females, aged 10 and upwards, are listed as being in employment. Apart from the influx of *Sais* (Englishmen) into the county, the census shows twenty-eight Americans, twenty-five Germans and twenty-one Russians resident in Flintshire.

The census can provide a vast amount of information to the researcher and can usually be accessed at your local library.

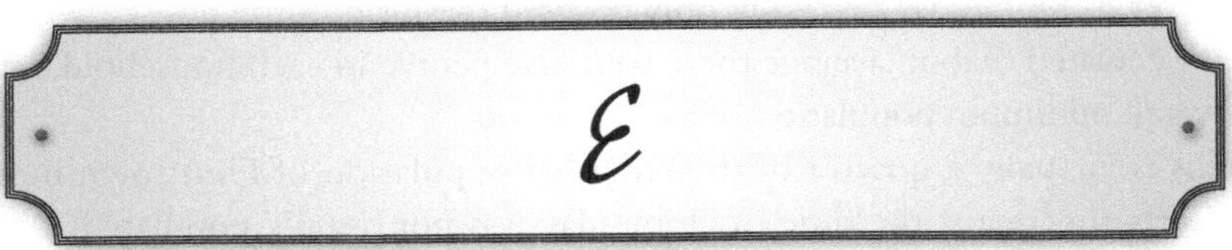

EISTEDDFODAU – MOSTYN SILVER HARP

The book by Thomas Pennant, *The History of Whiteford and Holywell*, contains the following extract related to the pictured silver harp. It tells of the concern regarding people purporting to be minstrels and other entertainers:

> By the Queene … Whereas it is come to the knowledge of the lorde president, and others of the said council, in our Marches of Wales, that vagrant and idle persons, naming themselves minstrels, rhymers and bards, are lately grown into such an intolerable multitude within the principality of North Wales, that not only gentlemen and others, by their shameless disorders , are often disquieted in their habitations … at Caroyes in our county of Flint, and that William Mostyn, esquire … have had the gift and bestowing of the silver harp …

The Eisteddfod Harp. (Dr Shaun Evans)

By the sixteenth century, the ancient bardic tradition was still outwardly flourishing, playing positive and functional roles in Welsh society. Flintshire's status as a foremost region for the production of bardic craftsmen had been demonstrated at the obscure Carmarthen eisteddfod of the 1450s, when the awards for master poet, harp player and declaimer all went to Flintshire men.

The two eisteddfodau held at the market town of Caerwys in 1523 and 1567/68 constituted the most ambitious attempts ever made to regulate professional bardic practice in Wales. The purpose of both eisteddfodau was to secure a prosperous future for the bardic tradition by separating the highly trained and accomplished practitioners of the traditional bardic crafts from those unskilled jokers and vagrants who caused a public nuisance by travelling around the countryside in search of money for their derisory rhymes. The former were graded and provided with a licence or degree allowing them to continue the practice of their crafts, whereas the latter group were dismissed and encouraged to adopt alternate professions.

In both 1523 and 1567/68, the head of the powerful Mostyn family played a major role in the organisation and adjudication of the events. The Mostyn family were fiercely proud of their Welsh heritage and fervent patrons of Welsh cultural activity. In 1523 Richard ap Hywel of Mostyn (*c.*1468–1540) was named as the chief commissioner and it was his grandson, William Mostyn (*c.*1521–76), who was instructed to make all the necessary preparations for the event in 1567/68. The original commission for the second eisteddfod, granted under the authority of Elizabeth I, still remains at Mostyn Hall. The pictured document states that 'William Mostyn Esquire and his ancestors had the gift and bestowing of the Silver Harp appertaining to the chief of the facultie'. This silver badge, the *ariandlws*, one of the national treasures of Wales, also remains in the possession of the family. As a further reminder of the symbolic importance of the eisteddfodau, the Caerwys town coat of arms and mayor's chain of office both contain the Mostyn Harp rising out of a 'bardic crown'.

EXCISE MEN AND COLLIERS WEARING FINE LINEN

Located on the A548 coast road, near Mostyn, will be found an alehouse once owned by the renowned naturalist and writer Thomas Pennant. Pennant called it 'Lletty Goneft', or the 'Boneft Boufe', but today it is known as Lletty Gonest. He describes how:

> The house was originally built by one Smith, from Worcester, partly for the purposes of distilling, and partly for a warehouse. I am told, that occasionally it had served as the place of confinement for impressed men and the strong bars in the lower windows favour that notion.

This was no doubt the reason the excise men chose the alehouse to store the confiscated liquor, as described in the following tale told by Pennant:

> In the reign of King William, this house was remarkable for the violent hands laid on a vast seizure of French wines, to the amount of sixty pipes (this quantity is a minimum of 475 litres), which had been smuggled into the great barn at Talacre, in the parish of Llanasa, destined for the use of the Welsh gentry in this and the neighbouring counties. It must be observed, that in those days port wine was very little used in our country. The Revenue officers had conveyed this prize with safety as far as the Llety Goneft, where they intended to sleep for the night. At midnight they were alarmed by the entry of multitudes of colliers, who tied everybody in the house neck and heels. They removed the wine into carriages, and conveyed it into places so secure that it never more could be heard of. Many of the colliers were observed to have rings on their fingers, and fine linen. In fact numbers of them were gentlemen interested in the wine, and concerned in the recapture who mixed with the colliers to direct them in their operations. A proclamation was issued for the discovery of offenders; but such was the fidelity of our people, that they were never detected. The poor tapster, in particular, knew perfectly well who they were, and large rewards were offered to him by the custom house; but nothing could shake his attachment to his friends. He lived long after, supported by the grateful contributions of the neighbouring squires.

Do the cellars of some of our country houses still contain some of this illicit 'port wine'?

EDUCATION, PARROTS AND THE LOGBOOK

We often hear the expression of teaching pupils 'parrot fashion'; well, in the nineteenth century, Bagillt and Gronant boasted of schools where parrots were taught to talk and sing!

However, it is the more traditional education of children that we are considering. Prior to the implementation of compulsory education, an 1847 census of Flintshire schools provided for the poor listed a total of sixty-five schools catering for 5,099 children. The Anglican Church ran sixty of these schools, for 4,893 children; Calvinistic Methodists provided one school for forty-eight children; Independents provided two schools for 103 children; and Roman Catholics ran two schools with fifty-five children.

The 1862 Revised Code of Regulations made the keeping of a logbook compulsory, and specified:

> The Principal Teacher must daily make in the Log Book the briefest entry which will suffice to specify either ordinary progress, or whatever other fact concerning the School or its Teachers, such as the dates of withdrawals, commencements of duty, cautions, illness, &c., may require to be referred to at a future time, or may otherwise deserve to be recorded.

C.H. Leslie in his 1869 book *Rambles around Mold* wrote: 'And, hark! What is that comes cheerily on this scene where we thought we were wandering in silence and loneliness? 'Tis the sweet voice of innocent childhood being dismissed from the school at Gwernaffield.' This sweetness and light is not always apparent from the Gwernaffield School logbook. School managers were expected to visit daily and records of such visits are included within the logbook. These books provide a wonderful insight into the lives of the families living in a mixed agricultural and mining area:

13 February 1863 – Attendance smaller on account of fair at Mold.
29 October 1863 – Fire first lighted in the Large School. Teachers finished reading the Bible to the end of the Second Book of Samuel, and as the attendance was very small on account of heavy rain, they are examined on the history and the Geography of the Holy Land.
18 April 1864 – Thomas Jones, Pantflas, on refusing to obey the master received a light slap on the cheek which caused him to do what he was told. In the absence of the master, his brother George Jones, persuaded the boy to go home and the next morning brought an impertinent note to the master who showed it to F. Phillips Esq. (of Rhual) who told the master to be cautious when using corporal punishment and severely reprimanded George Jones for his conduct. In the evening I took the note to Wm. Jones the boy's father and asked him what he means by sending me such a letter for I had done nothing improper to his child and told him what serious injury such a charge might do to a person in my situation. The note was quite strange to him – He said he saw nothing more than usual in Thomas. The note which (falsely) stated that the boy had fits was written by George Jones and his mother in the absence of Mr Jones. I cannot imagine from what cause Sarah Jones did such a thing unless it was to spite me because I had ordered George Jones to pay for a Ruler and two panes of glass in the Schoolroom which had broken through the bad behaviour of throwing stones and throwing things across the School. [George Jones was a pupil teacher and following various complaints about his absenteeism, behaviour, and lack of effort, the managers invited him to resign his post, an offer he accepted and was paid £5 in settlement.]
28 October 1864 – There was not much work done in School after 3 o'clock as many of the boys were taken out to put the coal in the coal-house and to clean the yard. Children cautioned to behave in Church and School on Sunday and to take warning from Edward Ellis who was punished on Monday for bad behaviour in Church last Sunday after repeated warnings.'
30 September 1867 – The attendance was small as a considerable quantity of corn is still out.

Similar low attendances were reported at various times in the agricultural calendar as children's labour was required in the fields.

It was not only essential work that kept children from school, as highlighted by a school manager, Basil Philips of Rhual, on 22 July 1900: 'I find the attendance very irregular and also find Wednesdays are worse than other days. The attendance officers would do well to look around the Auction yard in Mold on this day.'

As well as absences due to farming activity, schools were also badly hit by the spread of various infections:

> 21 October 1867 – a great decrease in attendance on account jointly of potato picking but most through the rapid spreading of the Scarlet Fever.

Five days later the school was closed for three months, and on 18 November 1867 the logbook entry confirmed the severity of such epidemics, in that five children had died from the fever. Over the following years, epidemics of whooping cough, chicken pox, diphtheria, mumps, German measles and measles struck the school, and the entry for 2 July 1917 records another death:

> Diphtheria and Whooping Cough have broken out, the former at Pantymwyn, the latter in the neighbourhood. Several families affected. Eveline Ledsham, one of our little scholars died today, after an illness of only a few days. She was present at School on Wednesday last and was one of our most promising pupils. School flag half mast.

Not all absences were the result of these infections as, in July 1923, Elizabeth Pickering was injured by the fall of the school bell and required an operation at Mold Cottage Hospital.

The issue of the Welsh language remained a thorny one, and the entry for 4 March 1868 states:'The children cautioned not to speak Welsh with one another

Sweet sound from Gwernaffield School. (Ray Davies)

especially on the School premises as all their instruction has to be imparted to them in the English Language.' In a predominately Welsh-speaking area it is no real surprise that the need to learn in a 'foreign' language should elicit this pre-examination entry: 'Scholars in Standard I will fail unless some extraordinary means be taken to bring them forward. Some of them were over seven years of age when lately admitted not knowing a letter or figure.'

The logbooks also contain a number of remarks on the question of discipline and the intervention of parents. The entry for 8 November 1906 is anything but complimentary: 'I find the discipline very lax, the behaviour of the children anything but desirable and their attainments of a very meagre character. It will take a long time to work the school up to a satisfactory level.' So very different from the HMI's report of May 1872: 'this is a first rate county school. The children presented for examination passed without a failure.'

The staff's efforts, in 1906, in bringing the children up to a satisfactory level were obviously not always appreciated by parents: 'Mrs Jones, mother of Rebecca Jones, entered the School without permission and behaved in an insulting way because her daughter was detained for Arithmetic. She said she was going to remove the pupil from the School.' Although Rebecca returned to the school, she was initially excluded until the managers had decided on a course of action. Their decision is recorded in the entry for 30 May 1907: 'The Vicar instructed me to receive the girl back and to write informing her mother that if she behaved in like manner again she would be summoned for trespass. The girl returned today.'

Throughout the logbooks, comments are made regarding the condition and cleanliness of the school, and the involvement of the children themselves in keeping the premises clean, as well as moving the coal required for the school fires. The school was heated by two stoves, and in February 1933 one of these almost resulted in a serious incident: 'At 9.45 this morning, volumes of smoke were noticed issuing from underneath one of the stoves. Investigation found the floorboards to be on fire. Prompt action was taken and a serious fire undoubtedly averted.'

The family of Rhual were closely involved with the school, both as managers and visitors, and children no doubt appreciated the annual treat of being taken to the 'big house' and being provided with tea and often an orange. The entry for 29 May 1945, records the visit by a member of the royal family: 'HRH Princess Royal visited at Rhual. The children of this School were invited to sing before Her Royal Highness. They sang "Ar hyd y nos" and "Llwyn Onn". The Princess thanked them and complimented them on their singing. A half days holiday was granted in celebration of the event.'

The requirement to maintain logbooks ceased in the late 1900s, and many schools no longer continue to maintain these, so we possibly have lost a useful source of research material for future generations.

FLINT PARISH CHURCH – THE STORY OF A STAINED-GLASS WINDOW

Jenkins' window. (Peter Bellis)

In the north wall of St Mary & St David parish church of Flint will be found a stained-glass window by Ward & Hughes, bearing a Latin inscription which translates as follows: 'To the Glory of the Blessed Trinity this window in memory of his benevolent servant in the ninth year of his ministry Evan Jenkins Rector of this Parish. Kind parishioners dedicated it to the Rector 1874.'

The rector of Flint from 1866–1874, during his ministry Evan Jenkins was described by his bishop as 'a diligent, conscientious and efficient clergyman', and he also had two church schools built during his incumbency. Unfortunately, he also had a running dispute with the Bishop of St Asaph, who had ordered that the language of the evening service be changed from English to Welsh. The language issue would come back to trouble Jenkins in his later ministry.

The other major issue that blighted his life resulted in the bishop's withdrawal of an offer to the vacant living of Holt in 1875 because of his drinking habits. This particular episode came to a head when he and a fellow guest at a luncheon were both drunk and entered into a major quarrel. It is claimed that the withdrawal of the offer did have a sobering effect on Jenkins, such that in 1880 he was appointed rector of the parish of Manafon, Montgomeryshire, but the title of an article in the *Montgomeryshire Collections*, 83 (1995) gives an indication of what a turbulent time he had in this parish: 'Sad, Mad or Bad: the case of Evan Jenkins, Rector of Manafon.'

On his relocation to Manafon, the Welsh language issue re-emerged, as his bishop insisted that Welsh be used in services for what he said was a predominately Welsh-speaking population, a fact Jenkins disputed. Despite continued pressure from the bishop, it is believed that the Welsh-speaking Jenkins failed to comply with the instruction.

It also appears that Jenkins had not been particularly pleasant to parishioners, and he had committed offences against ecclesiastical law, by allowing the laity to conduct part of services. This particularly enraged one lady who, aware of the Holt issue, entered into an acrimonious correspondence with the Archbishop of Canterbury and the diocesan bishop.

Jenkins' failure to reduce his tithe entitlement also caused a further dispute with his parishioners, and all these factors appeared to once again have driven him back to his old drinking habits. So much so that in the late 1880s the living was sequestered, and Jenkins subsequently spent a number of years in various mental asylums. The *Manchester Times*, dated 10 April 1891, ran the following article:

> In regard to the paragraph with reference to the Bishop of St Asaph's mention to the Rev. Evan Jenkins M.A. rector of Manafon, Montgomeryshire, it is now explained that Mr Jenkins has been in ill-health for some time, and left his parish with the sanction of the Bishop.

Following his discharge from the Virginia Water Asylum in 1892, it is quite clear from his actions that he still suffered mental health problems, as he then embarked upon a series of personal attacks against all he believed had wronged him and this included his cousin, the Reverend Edward Jenkins. His alleged crime was to have him incarcerated in order to take possession of various insurance policies.

Despite these actions he was readmitted to his parish in late 1892, but his health and drinking habits had not improved. The *Liverpool Mercury* headlined on 7 February 1893: 'A Welsh Rector charged with drunkenness'. Found guilty of being drunk and disorderly, this was followed with further appearances in court on similar charges and also of assaulting a police officer and using vile and profane language. In April 1893, newspapers reported that he unsuccessfully applied for a summons to be taken out against his cousin, Reverend Edward Jenkins, and Mr Bennett Rowlands 'charging them with attempting to confine him in Shrewsbury Lunatic Asylum and ultimately to kill him so as to obtain insurance money to the amount of £500'.

In 1892, the Clergy Discipline Act came into force and, as reported by many national and local newspapers in May 1893, the Disciplinary Commission found him guilty of various charges and he was accordingly 'Dismissed and deprived of all profits, and benefits, and other ecclesiastical dues, rights, and emoluments appertaining to the rectory and parish church'.

In October, of the following year, we find the Chester Board of Guardians considering charges of conspiracy, made by Jenkins against the Medical Officer of Health and the Relieving Officer. This once again centred on insurance policies, this time valued at £200. The two were accused 'of a diabolical project entering the men's minds of capturing him with a view to killing him in private asylums … a Bishop was also implicated in the plot and there was a systematic plot to kill him'.

This is not the end of the story, as in 1899 he reappears in various parishes as a curate before finally returning to Flint around 1906. He died in 1916, and is buried in North Road cemetery. This brought to an end the troubled life of a person so well respected by his Flint parishioners that a memorial window was dedicated to him.

FLINTSHIRE PLANTS

A survey was launched in 2002 to mark the Queen's Golden Jubilee and also to highlight the threat to Britain's wildflowers. Plantlife held a nationwide poll, with the public being invited to vote for a wildflower emblem for their county. Flintshire people apparently chose the bell heather (*Erica cinerea*) which produces a blaze of colour on the moors at the end of summer.

Flintshire's plant. (Carl Rogers)

Whilst the bell heather is highly visible, the hunt is on to discover whether a Flintshire gooseberry is fact or fiction. To date, attempts to discover whether such a plant existed have all come to naught. It is believed that if it did exist it would have survived in hedgerows, and samples from local hedgerows were sent for analysis to the National Fruit Centre in Brogdale, Kent. Unfortunately the analysis was inconclusive and, whilst Denbighshire have traced a plum unique to the county, we have still to discover the truth about the Flintshire gooseberry.

GATES THAT NEVER OPENED

Sir George Wynne (1700–1756) was the son of a relatively poor country gentleman who had the good fortune to inherit, from his mother Jane, a field in Halkyn which was found to contain valuable lead deposits. After a prolonged dispute with his father and the Grosvenor estate over the mineral rights, George set about spending his newly found extensive wealth.

Leeswood Hall was built around 1724–26, and attributed to Francis Smith, an architect of Warwick. The house (now greatly reduced) originally had eleven bays, with a third storey above the main cornice, and side wings of thirteen bays each. It is believed to have cost in the region of £40,000, a huge sum at that time. The famous landscape architect Stephen Switzer designed the garden and the crowning glory were two sets of wrought ironwork gates – the Black Gates

Leeswood Hall's White Gates. (Eric Keen)

(now at Tower) and the magnificent White Gates (believed to have cost in the region of £1,500). These were manufactured by renowned craftsmen – either the Davies brothers of Bersham, or possibly Robert Bakewell of Derbyshire. Local legend has it that the gates were never paid for and therefore never opened, but sadly this was not the case.

George Wynne served as High Sheriff of Flintshire from 1722–24, and was Constable of Flint Castle from 1734–50. Awarded a baronetcy in 1731, and under the premiership of Horace Walpole, he represented Flint Boroughs in Parliament during the years 1734–42. Not everyone was impressed with the gentleman, as voiced by this comment from the renowned traveller, Mrs Hester Lynch Thrale: 'He was a beacon kept burning by Providence I guess in order to warn others from *frantick* and *extravagante expence*. George Wynne was a low born lad … Gentlemen contributed money towards putting him to school, but he was a dunce and could be taught nothing.'

The expense of the elections and building programme left Wynne with extensive debts, and he found himself incarcerated in the Kings Bench Debtors Prison in London. Even then he could not escape the caustic tongue of Mrs Thrale, who commented, 'having leave to walk out [from prison] on Sundays, when I have seen him in the park many times, and considered him a creature permitted by Providence to warn mankind of the dangers incurred by sudden and unmerited riches'. However, we need to thank the man who left us with the wonderful legacy of the black and white gates.

GOLF HOLE THAT DISAPPEARED

In November 1958, two golfers were approaching the second hole on Mold Golf Course, with one player having chipped his second shot onto the raised green and the other looking to play his third shot from just off the green. To their amazement there was no sign of the ball on the green – indeed, there was no sign of the green itself! There was, however, the noise of running water.

It appears that the green had been constructed on a mound of soil left over from lead mining which, in turn, was over a disused mineshaft. The heavy rain of that autumn had loosened the soil, with the resultant collapse of the green. Remedial work was subsequently carried out and the green is now the fifth hole in the current course layout, and players once again have to resort to putting into a 4in hole rather than the significantly larger one caused by the collapse.

Mind you, this was not the only hazard players were faced with at this particular hole. On 3 October 1940, a Hawker Hurricane from RAF 17 Squadron, piloted by Sergeant Glyn Griffiths, made a 'wheels up forced landing' close to what is now the fifth tee.

The danger caused by collapsed mine workings is not just confined to Mold Golf Club. In the *Halkyn Mountain News* (Autumn 2012) details were given of shallow mine workings which collapsed on Holywell Golf Course. Over 4,000 mining shafts are believed to be found on the Holywell Common, and a couple of years ago, a major shaft collapsed behind the now closed school, Ysgol Rhes-y-cae.

GHOSTS AND THE MYSTERY PILOT

The county has no shortage of ghost stories, with Plas Teg considered to be the most haunted house in Wales. In 2009, the paranormal society Spirit Quest UK claimed to have detected twenty spirits in Tower, the fifteenth-century castellated house on the outskirts of Nercwys. The spirits included an Edwardian gentleman, a nursemaid and a dog, but surprisingly not the Mayor of Chester who, it was claimed, was hanged in the house during the fifteenth century.

The Party Shop in Mold High Street has a mysterious figure of a girl peering through a window overlooking Earl Road. Did 'Sara' die from smallpox? Did she commit suicide? Or was the servant girl pregnant, murdered and thrown down the deep well in the cellars? At times she makes her presence felt, as does the mysterious presence in the Country Casual/Viyella shop in Mold High Street.

Many public houses have both kinds of spirits, but the various hauntings related to the Black Lion at Babell mark this out from others as it claims a variety of strange happenings throughout its long history. The clock has come off the wall, glasses fall for no apparent reason, the music volume goes up and down without explanation, and amongst the figures experienced is a lady called 'Annie' who is seen wearing a long back dress with an apron.

However, it is one story that provided the strangest outcome. A landlord in the 1970s rang the local police station to complain that someone with an American accent was shouting 'Help me!', and hammering on the door of the closed pub. The police advised him to open the door and see if he could help, to which the landlord replied he couldn't 'because there's no one there'. The police attended the scene, but by the time they arrived the noises had ceased and no explanation was forthcoming.

In 2011, North Wales Paranormal Society carried out a five-hour investigation into paranormal activity within the pub, and came up with the following explanation: the man was not an American, but Canadian. His first name seemed to go with the surname of Khan, and his second name suggested he was of Scandinavian descent. He had crashed a plane and been killed, but this episode was a 'play on time' as he did not realise he was dead and so he headed for the first light he had seen.

Do you believe such a story, and the experience of the society member?

The excellent book *Wings across the Border* records a 1940 crash of an RAF Oxford plane, flight number R6019, travelling from Prestwick to Kidlington, in Oxfordshire, with a stopover at RAF Hawarden. In poor visibility it crashed, coming to rest in the Glebe Field at Brynford crossroads with the pilot and two RAF passengers all being killed. The pilot, a flying officer, was a naturalised Canadian, but a Dane by birth, and his name was Aaga Valemar Helstrop Laursen. His grave can be found in St Deiniol's churchyard, Hawarden. So, remember the result of the paranormal investigation? Aaga to go with Khan, and of course the Scandinavian surname – a pure coincidence? Good prior research by the society member? Or a true paranormal experience?

GLADSTONE, THE MAD COW AND THE MORE THAN LIBERAL VISITORS

On 29 August 1892 the 'grand old man of politics', William Ewart Gladstone, was attacked by a heifer in Hawarden Park and a local man, Tom Bailey, was called on to shoot the unfortunate beast. Tom Bailey was a builder, parish councillor, the proprietor of the Castle Inn from 1876 until 1921, and a marksman in the Denbighshire Hussars. The head of the heifer was displayed in the Castle Inn before being moved to the Glynne Arms Hotel, from where it subsequently went missing. Its whereabouts remain a mystery.

The village of Hawarden, being the home of W.E. Gladstone, was a Mecca for organisations with similar political views. On 6 July 1893, 315 people of the Norwich Liberal Association visited and partook of a pre-ordered tea at the Glynne Arms. To accommodate the large number of people, the tea was laid out in a large tent erected inside Hawarden Park gates, opposite the hotel. The price agreed was 1*s* per head for a meal of bread and butter, cake and salad, although the organisers had attempted to have this supplemented with fruit as they considered 1*s* 'a bit stiff'.

A delay in serving the tea occurred, 'by reason of the milk having turned sour in consequence of the heat, and requiring to be replaced by a fresh yield from a number of hastily solicited cows'. After the tea was over, the landlord, Richard Darbyshire, noticed that many of the people were in a prone position at the edge of the tent, and at length it dawned upon him that they were crawling under the canvas, with the view of evading payment for the tea! He called the police, who brought several of the runaways back, and called upon them to show their tickets. With this assistance he managed to collect 295 tickets, leaving at least twenty-five not paid for.

Subsequently, he took the organisers to Chester County Court, and the defence offered that the supply of food was insufficient, which Richard indignantly denied, alleging, on the contrary, that many of the pilgrims filled not only their stomachs, but their pocket handkerchiefs, and were 'caught by the waitress skulking off with everything they could collect off the tables'. Other witnesses were called to corroborate the plaintiff's testimony. His son deposed that one of the trippers declared 'he had had no tea' – using the word, we presume, in the sense, not as a beverage but of a meal – when the assertion was refuted, so to speak, from his own lips by the damming evidence of jam on his moustache. A police sergeant stated that the people behaved in a very rough manner, and that, 'though the cake was crumbly through being handled, it was well baked, and there was plenty left after the party had gone'.

In vain did the defendant's witnesses strive to make out that the tea was poor in quality, that the jam did not look pleasant, that the salad consisted of a few leaves of lettuce, and that the bread and butter 'was only fit for a Sunday School treat'. The judge at Chester County Court refused to listen to these unworthy afterthoughts, and was especially scandalised by a remark of one of the defendant's witnesses that 'he should not like to have been left behind in that wild part of the world'. Judgement was given for the plaintiff, with costs.

GRAVESTONES, GYPSIES AND METHODISTS

Located in St Matthew's churchyard, Buckley, is the headstone for Hannah Krohn, aged 2 years 8 months, who died on 15 August 1876. In the nineteenth century, gypsies often visited Buckley to buy local pottery to sell during their travels around the country. During one such visit the daughter of one family died and, whilst death in childhood was nothing unusual during the nineteenth century, the quality of the headstone reflects the loss of their daughter by a devoted family. What also makes this special is that the headstone is made of pottery and produced by a local Buckley potter. Whilst all the pottery workshops have now closed, this memorial to a much-loved child remains as a testament to the quality of the local workmanship.

A gravestone found in Ysceifiog churchyard tells a totally different story. Throughout the centuries it appears that adherents of particular religions, and even groupings within a particular branch, have displayed antagonistic – sometimes violent – tendencies towards other forms of Christianity, and this is true of Flintshire. With Christianity, the action of Henry VIII splitting from Rome subsequently resulted in some very bloody periods in our history. Equally, when Nonconformists started their activities, this was not welcomed by members of the established Church. But how many of us would dream of making our feelings known on our gravestones?

Hugh Hughes, whose grave can be found in Ysceifiog churchyard, has the following engraved on his headstone:

Here lyeth the body of the late Hugh Hughes, Coed-y-Brain. In the hope of blessed Resurrection he had the Honour in 1743 to serve the public in the office high *sheriffe* for his county. In private life his manner was constantly to attend the Public Worship as by Law established heavily to declare against the upstart sect of Brainsick Methodists that would take men off from it …

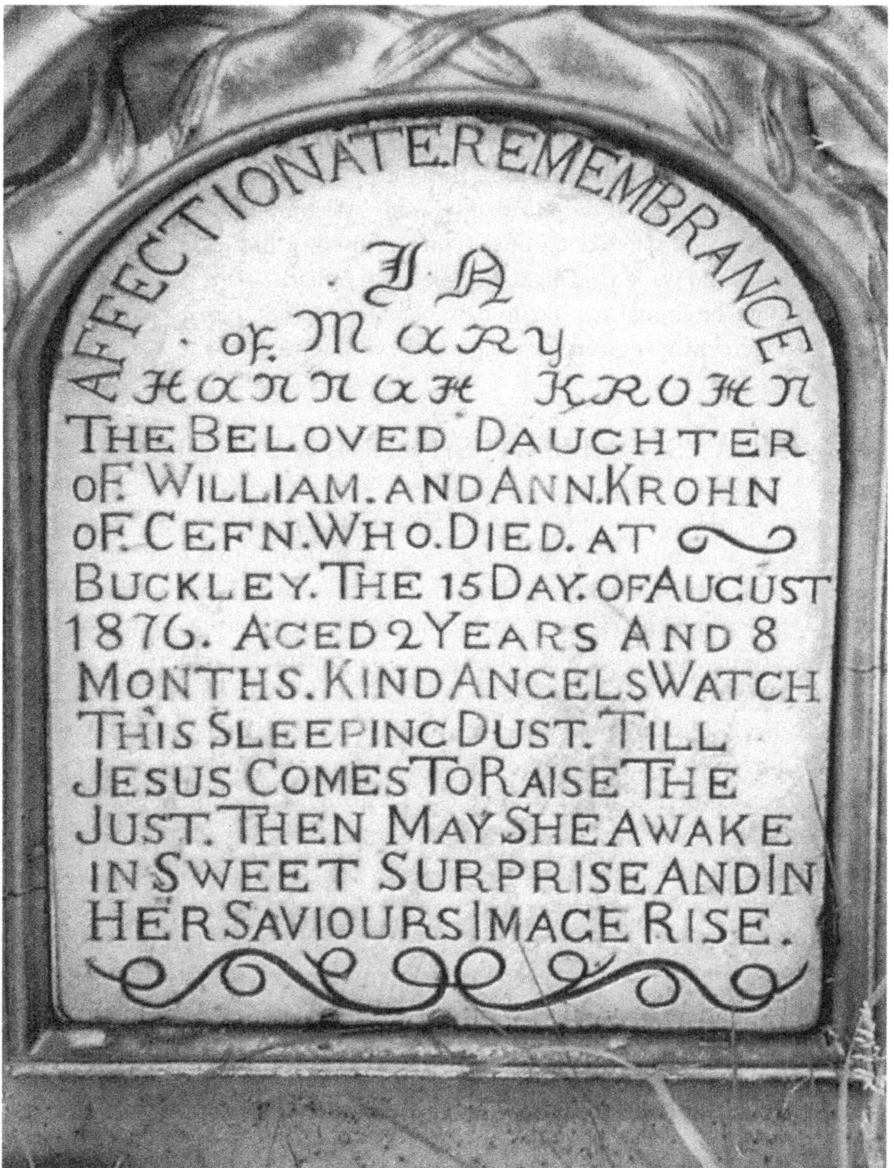

The pottery grave. (Paul Davies)

H

HATCHMENT – SIR ROGER MOSTYN

A hatchment is a funerary plaque normally displaying the coat of arms and other heraldic symbols of the deceased and is usually placed against the wall of their house. After a defined period of time, six or twelve months, it was often then installed in the parish church. However, a family feud between Sir Thomas and his son, Sir Roger Mostyn, resulted in a hatchment with a totally different purpose.

Sir Thomas Mostyn died in 1618 and is buried in the parish church of Whitford – his will, dated 10 December 1617, contained bequests to both male and female servants at both the family homes, Mostyn and Gloddaeth, in Llandudno. During his lifetime Sir Thomas Mostyn (*c.*1542–1618), as a prerogative of his noble ancestry, had moulded himself into an exemplar of Welsh gentility, maintaining a massive landed powerbase, carving out a pre-eminent office-holding career and asserting his status, leadership and authority on communities across North Wales. In spite of these achievements, his relationship with his eldest surviving son and heir, Sir Roger Mostyn (*c.*1568–1642), had been ridden with tension, especially since Sir Roger's marriage in 1596 to Mary, the daughter of Sir John Wynn of Gwydir.

Reporting from Sir Thomas Mostyn's deathbed at Mostyn Hall in February 1618, Sir Roger Mostyn stated that his father was 'never more malitious towards my wyeff and me … greetinge not at our beinge heare'. Indeed, via his last will and testament, Sir Thomas Mostyn had essentially attempted to disinherit his eldest son. Sir Thomas Mostyn's funeral was held at Whitford church in March 1618. Far from representing a ceremony designed to commemorate the deceased, Sir Roger Mostyn sought to take centre stage at the event, using it to override his father's wishes and propagate his rightful claim to dynastic succession. Indeed, Sir Thomas Mostyn's body was not even present at the funeral, it having already been buried. The heraldic funeral procession – like so many seventeenth-century gentry funerals in North Wales – was organised by the Randle Holme workshop of Chester, which was also largely responsible for the instigation of this region's portraiture tradition.

One of the funeral hatchments paraded at Sir Thomas Mostyn's funeral, and produced by the Randle Holme workshop, features the coat of arms of Sir Roger Mostyn, conjoined with those of the Wynns of Gwydir. This powerful

The hatchment of Sir Thomas Mostyn. (Dr Shaun Evans)

heraldic display demonstrated to all present that Sir Roger Mostyn was now in control of the Mostyn family and, in spite of Sir Thomas Mostyn's hostility towards this union, the lineage would prosper as a result of his noble alliance with the Wynns of Gwydir. Funerals *are* for the living rather than the dead!

Following Sir Thomas Mostyn's funeral, Sir Roger Mostyn proceeded to plaster the heraldic iconography of his marriage throughout his new residence of Mostyn Hall. The hatchment referred to above, and as pictured, will be found hanging in Mostyn Hall today.

HOME GUARD, OR 'LONG DENTURED VETERANS' (LDV)

The Home Guard totalled about 1.7 million men at its peak, and locally the guard came under the Mid-west, No. 4 Clwydian Range Sector and No. 5, Dee Valley, Cambrian Sub-District, comprising of seven battalions.

We all remember the favourite line from the TV series when the German submarine captain asks for the soldier's name, and the inept Captain Mainwaring shouts, 'Don't tell him, Pike!' Well, was it really like this in the Home Guard, or, would the 'Dad's Army' really have proved a match for the battle-hardened, highly trained, German troops who would have been involved in the invasion of Britain?

The guard was originally called the Local Defence Volunteers (LDV), or alternatively 'Look, Duck and Vanish', 'Long Dentured Veterans' or 'Last Desperate Venture'. In one recorded case, a solitary patroller spotted a suspicious character in the middle of a field, challenged him and, having received no reply,

Home Guard uniform. (David Rowe)

fired only to find he had shot a scarecrow. The stories told by one 90-years-plus ex-Home Guard soldier, Len Buckley, who was 18 years old when he enlisted, will enable you to make our own mind up.

Len was paralysed as a child, and when he volunteered to join the regular forces he failed the medical and, much to his disgust, the medical officers told him 'you are no good to us'. He subsequently enlisted in the 5th Battalion (Flintshire-Hawarden) of what was then the Local Defence Volunteers. They were based at Drill Hall, in Connah's Quay. For clothing they had some cast-off pieces of uniform, and initially an LDV arm band.

They were on duty every night, and training generally took the form of talks, or static drills, whereas Len thought they should be trained to be partisans and learn to fight in the streets. As part of their duties, they were required to guard a particular location on the shore of the River Dee. However, it was soon realised that that their position on a knoll silhouetted them against the sky, so they dug a square hole in which they stood guard.

Whilst on duty one night, Len heard a bang down amongst the fishing boats and shouted, 'Who goes there?' Having received no reply, he fired a shot and, whilst lots of scrambling followed, the source of the bang was not discovered, although they suspected it was a man with a very strange habit. Somewhere in Connah's Quay a man used to run about naked every night, and the police and the Home Guard looked out for him, but he was never caught, nor his identity discovered.

Whilst the Home Guard were armed, Len pointed out that it was very rare that they were given ammunition. However, on one occasion when they did have live ammunition he came off guard, and had climbed into his bunk when a corporal, a First World War veteran, tested a rifle on the rack and it discharged into the wall above his head. Len commented, 'I have never moved so quickly as I dived under the bunk.' One wonderful tale that sums up the local organisation is best told using Len's own words:

> One Saturday night we were ordered to a 'Quays' exercise with Northop Hall and, about 20 of us with a red haired and unpopular Sergeant in command, marched off up the Mold Road onto a lane, and then across fields, until we came to the outskirts on the east side of the village. The Sergeant stopped us at a gate and said 'beyond here is a lane. When I give the order, climb the gate, run across the lane and jump the little wall'. I protested, as I was aware there was a big drop on the other side, but was told to shut up in no uncertain terms. The order was given so they all raced across the lane, jumped the wall landing on top of each other. They lost their rifles, and helmets, and you would be able to hear the noise from miles away. I was the last to the wall, so I slung my rifle and lowered myself over it. In the dark it took a long time to get everyone together and we set off across the field to prepare to ambush the Northop Hall unit. When we got to the gate, we found ourselves surrounded by the Northop Hall unit who 'arrested' us and told us we were going to be locked up. As we were marched down the lane, near Northop Hall Cricket Club, six heads appeared over the wall pointing their rifles and started jeering us. I pulled out a hidden pistol from my back pocket, (loaded with blanks) and fired at each of them, whereupon they, and the others escorting us, just disappeared. I was told in no uncertain terms that I had wrecked the whole exercise and it could not proceed any further. When I reported for duty on Monday evening, they were waiting for me and I was put before the CO, Capt. Bob Jones, and received a right telling off and I thought they would throw me out. The Captain told me 'I had no business to carry that weapon so why do you as it is not sporting?' My reply was quite simple 'because I like it so I can fight Germans when they come'. I was not popular but was allowed to remain in the unit.

Len's interest in firearms continued, and post-war he became an expert on antique firearms, so much so that the police often consulted him. With Len being the character he is, there are many more examples of his eccentricity. Celebrating a significant birthday party in a hotel, attended by a number of senior police officers, he suddenly produced a number of antique firearms, albeit deactivated, totally oblivious to the fact that this alarmed the hotel staff, who were about to ring the police armed response unit. Fortunately a very embarrassing situation was avoided when one of the policeman explained the situation.

J

INDENTURES

Indentures were a contractual document between an apprentice and his master (the tradesman), and failure to meet the terms left the apprentice liable to legal action, including possible imprisonment. To portray yourself as a time-served tradesman if you were not was also an offence punishable by law. Two copies of indentures were normally made, one of which was kept by the parents (or parish/poor union) and the other by the master. The standards of behaviour and restrictions on the apprentice, along with the duties of the master, are clearly defined in this extract from the 1890 indenture of Joseph Dykins of Mold to Joseph Vaughan, a Mold blacksmith:

> Unto the full End and Term of Five Years from thence next following to be fully complete and ended. During which Term the said Apprentice his Master faithfully shall serve his secrets keep his lawful commands every where gladly do He shall do no damage to his said Masters nor see to be done of others but to his Power shall tell or forthwith give warning to his Masters of the same He shall not waste the Goods of his said Master nor lend them unlawfully to any person shall not contract Matrimony within the said Term nor play at Cards or Dice Tables or any other unlawful Games whereby his said Master may have any loss with his own goods or others during the said Term without Licence of his said Master He shall neither buy nor sell shall not haunt Taverns or Playhouses not absent himself from his said Masters service day or night unlawfully. But in all things as a faithful Apprentice he shall behave himself towards his said Master and all his during the said Term. And the said Joseph Vaughan hereby covenants and agrees to pay the said Apprentice the sum of Two Shillings per week during the first two years of the said term, Four Shillings during the Third year of the said term and Seven Shillings per week during the Fourth and Fifth year of the said term provided the said Apprentice is able to follow his employment and the said Robert Dykins hereby covenants and agrees to keep the said Joseph Dykins with Board and Lodgings, and the said Joseph Vaughan further covenants to teach his said Apprentice in the Art of a Blacksmith in all its branches which he uses by the best means that he can shall teach and Instruct or cause to be taught and instructed.

What would today's employment human rights legislators, or the European Courts of Justice, make of such contracts of employment?

INSPECTOR CONQUEST OF SCOTLAND YARD AND THE PRIME MINISTER'S HAT AND COAT

During the premierships of W.E. Gladstone, there was real concern over the threat to his life from Fenians, and as the Flintshire Constabulary was not really experienced in personal protection, two armed police officers were despatched from Scotland Yard.

One of the officers was the wonderfully named 'Conquest of the Yard', and much later he is described in an article in *The North Norfolk Railway*, with its Sandringham link to the royal family, as being 'Poirot-style'. Born in 1850, he served in the police force for twenty-eight years and, in 1882, he was given special responsibility for the protection of the 'Grand Old Man'. During his long and distinguished career he solved a number of high profile cases, including a series of twenty robberies involving a Raffles-type character. This particular thief targeted the wealthy in London, and burgled ladies' bedrooms whilst the family were downstairs enjoying dinner.

Whilst he was certainly a serving policeman during the 'Ripper' murders, he does not appear to have been involved in the investigations. However, he was present at the retirement presentation of the senior investigating officer, Chief Inspector Abberline. However, it is work related to W.E. Gladstone that provided the national and local press with the most column inches. The *Liverpool Mercury* of 2 June 1884 records the 10-mile journey of Mr Gladstone, accompanied by Mrs Gladstone and Reverend Stephen Gladstone, from Hawarden via Ewloe to visit the Grosvenor family at Halkyn Castle. Their carriage was followed by another 'conveyance' containing Deputy Chief Constable Bolton, Inspector Aplin and Detective Conquest. A far cry from the multi-vehicle convoy that accompanies the current prime minister.

Conquest of the Yard. (Susan Phillips)

One story that did not appear in the press, at least initially, was the disappearance and subsequent death of Zadoc Outram, aged 38, Mr Gladstone's faithful valet. Zadoc was born in Liverpool and started work in 1870, aged 16, as a footman for the Gladstones and was promoted to valet around 1881, travelling with the family on their many national and overseas trips. He developed a number of personal problems, including drinking issues, so although he was considered one of the family, it was no longer considered suitable for him to visit other people's homes.

The family arranged for him to have treatment at the Keeley Institute in London, and then following discharge he had a prolonged holiday before returning to work in Downing Street. A week after his return he disappeared, and Inspector Conquest was put in charge of the investigation. Ten days later, in December 1893, Conquest reported to Downing Street that Zadoc's body had been found in the River Thames. The newspapers were full of the story, and assumptions were made as to the reason for him going missing and the cause of death. The inquest jury, under guidance, returned a verdict of 'found drowned but there was no evidence to show how he got into the water'. So does the short note from Lord Rosebery to Catherine Gladstone give the real cause of death? 'I am sorry that in a fit of temporary insanity caused probably by the nervous system, Zadoc has made an end of himself.' The body was brought back to Hawarden where the funeral took place.

The night-time sojourns of the 'grand old man' have been well publicised, and it was more than likely that Mr Gladstone was not happy about being shadowed by John Conquest. The *Daily Chronicle* of 28 October 1899 carried an article on Conquest's impending retirement with a story related to Mr Gladstone. On one occasion, whilst at his club, Gladstone persuaded a friend to walk out of the club wearing his unmistakeable hat and coat, and carrying his umbrella. However, the good inspector was not fooled, and following the gentleman outside he tapped him on the shoulder and said, 'I believe sir, you have just left that club with another gentleman's property in your possession'.

John Conquest was described in an article in a London journal as 'a terror to criminals, and that he has earned the right to be respected by all just and honest men'. His daughter, Emily, married Henry Darbyshire of the Glynne Arms, Hawarden, and we will hear more of Henry later in the book.

INVENTORS AND ENTREPRENEURS

We are all aware of the importance manufacturing once had in the county, from the early mills of Greenfield Valley, the copper bottom for HMS *Victory* from the Williams Copper Works at Greenfield, Summers Steelworks, Courtauld's, Airbus and the high technology of the author's pre-retirement company, Remsdaq Limited. However, without inventors and entrepreneurs none of this would have been possible, and Flintshire has had a number of successful inventors and engineers.

Described as a pioneer motorist and inventor, James Jones was a native of Hawarden and served his time as an apprentice mechanic at Sandycroft Foundry. In 1894, he opened a bicycle shop in Mold called Jones Motor & Cycle Co. Ltd, and he installed electricity at his shop, the first in Mold to be lit by this medium. It was so popular that he also installed electricity at some of the local gentry's houses. With motor cars and motorcycles starting to come onto the market, he became the first local agent for cars.

Pursuing his motoring interests, he purchased a Beeston Humber single-seat motorised tricycle. The manufacturing company was established in 1872, and one of their tricycles was the only one to complete the 1896 London–Brighton Emancipation Run. The purpose of the run was not to celebrate anything to do with the electorate, but the raising of the speed limit to a mind-blowing 12mph! However, in order to allow his wife to accompany him, Jones designed and built a forecarriage for the trike, but the double load proved too much for the machine. He therefore turned his attention to overcoming the problem, and subsequently designed, manufactured and patented the first 'two speed gear and free engine'.

Turn of the screw. (Mervyn Foulkes)

The design and patent were subsequently sold to the Star Cycle Company (Wolverhampton), but Jones did not rest on his laurels. In 1908, he invented the 'tubeless connector', which had phenomenal sales worldwide. These connectors were particularly appreciated in hot climates, where rubber connectors often melted before being unpacked.

A native of Mold, Peter Roberts returned to the town following a successful business career in Manchester, and one of his patents was the pictured (page 68) star-like shoe device – when your heel wore down you simply rotated it! However, he did leave another major legacy that many will be familiar with today, the town hall in Earl Road, Mold. This has a foundation stone that tells us that it was laid on George V's Coronation Day in 1911. Peter Roberts, whose portrait hangs on the Mold Town Hall staircase, subsequently retired to Bournemouth, and his son, Captain Norman Roberts, lived in the family home, Bromfield Hall, until it was demolished. Norman Roberts continued with the family's interest in the rubber industry and in those days before the internet, he utilised the radio waves and would be described as a 'radio ham'.

The Harley family and their Mold garage were well known throughout the area, and Trevor achieved legendary status with the stocking and supply of parts for ageing vehicles. His brother, the late Vic Harley, spent most of his working life elsewhere before returning to his native town on retirement. Whilst many will remember Victor for his involvement with various local organisations, they may

£26 TV. (www.earlytelevision.org)

not be aware of his considerable engineering talent. In 1931, at the tender age of 12, he sent away for a kit which enabled him to assemble a working television set. Unfortunately we don't have a record of the television, but amongst the kits available at this time was the Plessey-manufactured 'Baird Televisor', costing in the region of £26.

The BBC first started broadcasting thirty-line television programming in September 1929, and a regular schedule was run for a few hours per week, but only after regular radio broadcasting was completed for the day. A December 1930 programme schedule informs the viewer that weekday morning transmissions were made between the hours of 11 and 11.30 a.m., and evening transmissions were only available on Tuesdays and Fridays, at the late hour of midnight until 12.30 a.m. The programmes being broadcast comprised of music, with the odd sketch, conjurer and even a demonstration of ballet dancing thrown in for good measure.

As performers were unused to this particular medium, Baird Television Limited produced a guide, 'Instructions for Actors', which included the advice that 'owing to the fact that facilities for reading material will be restricted, this must be memorised'. Even at this time, smoking was controlled for, whilst it was allowed where necessary for the performance, 'a match must not be lighted in the studio'. Perhaps also conscious of the censor, all material had to be forwarded in advance. There also appeared to be a copyright issue, in that works by certain writers and composers, including Kipling, Novello and Gilbert & Sullivan were among those not available for broadcasting. (My thanks to the Early Television Museum for the information on early televisions, and if you want more information, check out their website www.earlytelevision.org.)

J

JESUITS, A CAB AND THE COUNTY GAOL

Many people will be aware that just across the county border into Denbighshire will be found St Beuno's Ignatian Spirituality Centre, Tremeirchion – the home of a community of Jesuits, or more correctly, the Society of Jesus. The college was designed and built in 1848 by Joseph Aloysius Hansom, who is probably better known for his 'Hansom Cab'. Amongst St Beuno's many past students was the renowned poet Gerald Manley Hopkins who, whilst studying theology at the college in 1874 also learnt Welsh. It is said that he adapted the rhythms of Welsh poetry into his own verse. The first two lines of his poem 'In the Valley of the Elwy' express his feelings towards the area:

> Lovely the woods, waters, meadows, combes, vales,
> All the air things wear that build this world of Wales

It is also fitting that Hopkins should write about St Winefride's Well at Holywell, as a Jesuit presence existed in the town from the late sixteenth century until 1930. Over the years, and despite persecution during various anti-Catholic periods, the Jesuits continued with their ministry. The early Jesuits operated out of the Star Inn in Holywell, for which they were paying £60 per year, and the priests were closely watched and subjected to regular raids by the authorities. The survival of Catholicism in Flintshire was in no small part due to the work of the Jesuits.

St Beuno's College once again featured when, as a result of the fallout from France's defeat in the Franco-Prussian War (1870–71), French Jesuits were expelled from France. The defeat was put down to the type of education expounded by the Jesuits, who at that time remained a dominant force in education. They were subsequently forbidden from having any real involvement in teaching or educational institutions. Following continued harassment until 1880, one Jesuit college from Lyon relocated, with support from St Beuno's, to the old County Gaol in Upper Bryn Coch Lane, Mold. The gaol, replacing that at Flint Castle, was first used for prisoners in August 1870, and as well as providing cells, the gatehouse contained the governor's residence and accommodation for prison staff. The gatehouse, prison blocks, workshops, other ancillary buildings and the 'seven yards high' perimeter wall were designed by Messrs Martin and Chamberlain of Birmingham, at a total cost of £25,333 1*s* 9*d*.

However, when in 1878 the Home Office took over responsibility for prisons, the gaol was closed and the Flintshire authorities sought a buyer for the establishment. This coincided with the Jesuit search for suitable premises in which to house their exiled Lyon community and to open a training college. In 1880/81 they paid the sum of £3,500 for the gaol. Cells became studies and bedrooms, and the new college was initially called St Germanus. Germanus was a French bishop who had led the Britons in the famous local battle, at Maes Garmon, known as the Alleluia Victory, but clearly the community had second thoughts and changed its name to St David's College. The college clearly went from strength to strength as, in his 1889 guidebook on North Wales, C.S. Ward describes walking on the outskirts of Mold towards Ruthin:

> A little to the left of the road is a Jesuit College (formerly Mold Gaol) and, if our walk be taken in the afternoon, the number of clerically dressed trios taking their daily constitutional and speaking any language but English will suggest to us that it is in a flourishing condition.

Author, Seren and Bran outside St David's College. (Judith Rowe)

The college remained operational until 1897, when the Jesuit authorities remaining in Lyon decided that it was no longer required and the premises were put in the hands of the local estate agents, T.C. Adams. However, selling such an establishment was not an easy task and, in the meantime, other uses were sought for the building. The *County Herald* of 24 August 1906 reported a change of use:

> An important change is taking place at the large building known as the Jesuit College. For many years this building (originally erected as a gaol) has been used by the Jesuits as a college for the training of priests. Now, the priests are vacating the establishment, having decided to enter fresh quarters at Canterbury; and their place is being taken by a number of nuns, who are coming over from France. It is stated that these nuns will carry out laundry work at the College.

The order of nuns from Caen paid the Jesuits £8,000 for the premises. In 1910, St David's was taken over by an Irish order of nuns, 'Our Lady of Charity of Refuge', from Drumcondra, Dublin, and as well as their laundry business they also 'reclaimed, instructed and presented girls and women'. Subsequently, the premises were used as detention barracks for British soldiers during the First World War, and it was also a temporary home for the boys of the River Mersey-based industrial training ship, *Clarence*. This temporary home for the boys was required after a number of the trainees had set the *Clarence* on fire for the second of three occasions.

In September 1900, a reward of £1 was offered for the recapture of two boys, natives of London, who absconded from what was described as St David's Reformatory School. Apart from the usual physical and clothing description, an article in the *Police Gazette* also stated that they were good clarinet players, one in B flat and the other in E flat. This conjures up the wonderful image of these two absconders busking at the side of the road, in an effort to raise money for their fares back to London.

The link with Jesuits came to an end in 1924, when the *Wrexham and North Wales Guardian* advertised the sale of the property, 'by direction of the Spanish ecclesiastical authorities' of a 'Spanish Property sold In Mold'. It was purchased for £3,000 by a Liverpool ship owner, Richard Hughes, of the nearby Bryn Coch Hall. Many of the buildings were subsequently demolished and the dressed stone used to build new houses in Cheshire, but the gatehouse, workshop and laundry have been converted to private residences, and the perimeter wall remains intact.

JURIES, THE HOLY ROOD AND THE FATIGUED VAGRANT

The basic premise of being tried by one's peers is a fundamental part of the British legal system, and juries have been in existence for over 1,000 years. Initially, these were used to provide local knowledge rather than be decision makers but by the fifteenth century, juries had assumed their current role. Tony Robinson, on his programme *Crime and Punishment*, narrated a story related to Flintshire and suggested it may be one of the first trials by jury, which seems rather strange as it was a statue (rood) on trial!

Legend has it that in AD 946, during the reign of Gruffydd ap Conan, King of North Wales, there was a major drought and the good people of Harden (Hawarden) prayed to a statue of Mary, but this failed to provide the much-needed rainfall. Lady Trawst, the wife of the governor of Hawarden Castle, tried her luck by praying earnestly and long, but the fates conspired against her, as the statue fell upon her head and she was killed.

It was decided to try the rood for murder. A jury was summoned, who found the object guilty of wilful murder. The sentence was hanging, but it was pointed out that it was already dead and to burn the sacred image would have been considered sacrilege. It was therefore decided to drown it in the River Dee, and the tide carried it to Chester, where the Cestrians buried it at the point it was found and gave it the following inscription:

> The Jews their God did crucify,
> The Hardeners theirs did drown,
> 'Cos, with their wants she'd not comply,
> And lies under this cold stone.

The burial place is claimed to be in the centre of what we now know as the 'Roodee' and the site of Chester Racecourse. This story also appears in a number of publications – but is it true, or just a piece of anti-Welsh propaganda?

In the nineteenth century, juries were often comprised of the local gentry, who also sat as magistrates, so for the agricultural worker or miner on trial, such personnel can hardly be described as being their 'peers'.

There were lighter moments for juries, as reported in June 1900, when James Haigh from Birmingham was charged with being found in Glanaber, Hough Green, Chester, 'for an unlawful purpose'. The accused said 'he had only committed the offence with the object of getting a shelter in prison'. He had tramped with bleeding feet from Holywell Workhouse and felt thoroughly fatigued. After a week's rest in prison he now felt alright. The chief constable prosecuting stated, to great laughter, 'I hope you will get a little more rest'. Haigh didn't really get his wish as he was sentenced to two calendar months with 'hard labour'.

In contrast, inquest juries tended to be drawn from the townspeople, and very sadly many of the inquests involved the deaths of children. Often the victims were the children of single mothers, who were forced to foster their children to relatives or relative strangers. Many of these women were often left in an abject state of poverty by the errant fathers of their children, and the mother may well have been in Holywell Workhouse at some stage. One particular inquiry in 1876 involved a child of 5 months who was placed with a woman at a charge of 3*s* 6*d* per week, but when the boy died he only weighed 8lb.

A further case involved another child being fostered out to the mother's sister and being severely mistreated. Some injuries were caused by the child being held under a fire grate and the hot ashes dropping on to his body.

KINGS AND QUEENS

Staircases, Bedposts and Memorials

Flintshire, being situated in the marches, has always been of particular interest to royal families throughout the centuries and was constantly fought over by the Welsh and the English. During the final Conquest of Wales by Edward I, the castle at Flint, being a day's march from the English base at Chester, was the first of the ring of castles built by Edward I. The castle was also the scene of the deposition of Richard II, when he was handed over to Henry Bolingbroke who, in 1399, was crowned Henry IV. The event is recorded in Act II, Scene III of William Shakespeare's play *Richard II.*

Queen for Nine Days and Bromfield Hall

Moving on a few centuries, we come across another intriguing tale associated with the tussle for the throne.

Whilst the date of the building of the original Bromfield Hall, demolished in 1965, is not known, it is believed to have been sometime in the sixteenth century. A housing estate can now be found on the site, although the original lodge on Wrexham Road survives as a private home. Amongst the past residents are William Jones of Lloyd Jones Brewers, David Williams of Alyn Tinplate Works, F.B. Summers of the Steelworks family and Peter Roberts, who we heard of earlier in the book. However, it is William Beale Marston, who occupied the hall in 1874, who is responsible for one of the county's great mysteries.

Whilst in London on business, it is reported that he called in, by chance, to a sale in Whitehall, where he purchased a staircase for the hall. To accommodate this staircase, it was necessary to extend the house and build an imposing porch with massive stone columns. This led into an entrance hall, complete with a beautiful mosaic floor, which then extended through to a huge dining room and drawing room. The newly created landings were also used as a picture gallery. The timing of the alteration is confirmed by a date of 1874 cut into the stonework over the new arch to the front entrance. However, it does not appear that the alleged provenance of the staircase was established until a much later date.

The last resident of the hall prior to its demolition was Peter Robert's son, Captain Norman Roberts, described as a connoisseur of antiques and art. In 1965, he told *Deesider Magazine* that he had carried out intensive research and claimed the staircase was the one down which Lady Jane Grey, the Nine-Day Queen, and daughter-in-law of the ambitious Duke of Northumberland, was led to the scaffold.

As the execution of both Dudley and Jane was conducted in the open air, in the grounds of the Tower of London, is it likely the staircase was subsequently moved to Whitehall? Following the demolition of the hall, it has always been believed that the staircase was moved to the Portmeirion Italianate village. Having checked with the village authorities, they have found nothing in their archive to substantiate this belief, so, are both stories just urban myths?

Another mysterious piece of royal furniture leads us to Broughton …

Kingmaker and the King's Bedposts

Broughton is more commonly known today for its out-of-town shopping complex and its aircraft factory. The latter was built in 1937–39, and has manufactured a variety of aircraft including Second World War Wellington and Lancaster bombers, the wooden multi-combat role Mosquito, the twin-tailed jet-propelled Vampire, and latterly, the HS125 Executive Jet and wings for the European Airbus.

Opposite the factory and Hawarden Airport, will be found St Mary's church. Built in 1824, it is part of the Hawarden benefice, and due to its close proximity to the airport has a warning beacon mounted on the roof of the tower. The church, designed by the architect John Oates and built by the efforts of the rector of Hawarden, George Neville-Grenville, with various grants and donations from wealthy friends, is relatively modern. It does contain at least one historic and unusual feature, however.

On the Woodcarvers Guild website section titled 'History of four poster beds', reference is made to the four posts being used to support the west gallery of the church. These carved oak bedposts, complete with many heraldic features, are believed to be the posts of a 'king-size' bed belonging to Henry VII that was made at the time of his marriage to Elizabeth of York. It is also interesting that amongst the heraldic badges is that of the Neville family. Elizabeth of York was the grand-daughter of Cecily Neville and, to go full circle, the rector was a descendent of a branch of Warwick the Kingmaker's family. The mystery remains as to where did these posts come from? Did they come through the Neville link? Or was the bed, as has been put forward by the Reverend W.F. John Timbrell, already part of the Henry VII's furniture at Hawarden? In his article 'Altar Plate in the Church of St Mary, Hawarden' the Reverend Timbrell states, 'It is recorded that Henry VII, frequently visited his mother at Hawarden …'

George Neville-Grenville, the rector of Hawarden responsible for the building of the church, subsequently held the prestigious position of Dean of Windsor. He was also a member of the Roxburghe Club. This was formed in 1812 by the

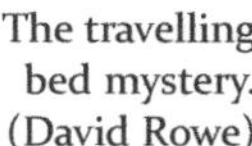

The travelling bed mystery. (David Rowe)

3rd Duke of Roxburghe and is the oldest society of bibliophiles in the world. Membership is limited to forty and each member is expected to produce a book, on any subject, at their own expense and present it to fellow members. Although these can also be purchased by the general public, prices are out of the reach of many people. Membership is chosen from amongst those with distinguished libraries or collections, or with a scholarly interest in books. The original members were all friends drawn from the ranks of the nobility, the professional and academic classes. Current members include the Duke of Devonshire, Mark Getty, the Duke of Northumberland, Lord Rothschild and most surprisingly, elected in 2011 was Dame Edna in her other guise, Barry Humphries.

The final link in this trilogy takes us to the Victorian age …

Flintshire's Link with Victoria and Albert's Sculptor

Born in Trentham, Staffordshire, William Theed the Younger (1804–1891) was the son of a painter and sculptor, William Theed the Elder. Initially trained by his father, he went on to work in the studio of E.H. Bailey and studied at the Royal Academy Schools. In 1826 he went to Rome, studying under a number

Theed and Gwernaffield. (David Rowe)

of renowned sculptors, and developed his particular talent by working in marble. Around 1844–45, he received a commission from Prince Albert and provided two statues for Osborne House on the Isle of Wight. Returning to London, in 1848, he established a successful career and was a great favourite of the royal family.

He displayed more than eighty works at the Royal Academy, and amongst his works is a bronze statue of Sir Isaac Newton and the 'Africa Group' on the Albert Memorial, opposite the gates of Buckingham Palace. So what, you may ask, is the link with Flintshire? At the rear of Holy Trinity church, Gwernaffield, can be found a signed white marble memorial to the Lloyd family of Leghorn (Livorno on the western coast of Tuscany, Italy) and Hafod (now the Plas Hafod Hotel). The memorial has the words:

> This monument was originally executed
> In memory of JOHN and JANE children of
> THOMAS LLOYD of Leghorn
> They died on 23 and 25 September 1842
> It is now placed in this church

There remains a mystery as to how this ended up in Holy Trinity which, although originally built in 1838, was subsequently destroyed by fire and rebuilt in 1871. Amongst the donors was a Mr Lloyd of the now demolished Cefn Mawr at Cadole. So the mystery remains as to whether this was originally produced, and installed, somewhere in Leghorn, and then subsequently relocated to its current location.

Locally, another piece of Theed's work can be found in All Saints' church, Gresford.

KNIGHT OF THE ORDER OF THE GARTER

Founded by Edward III in 1348, the Order of the Garter is the most senior and oldest British Order of Chivalry. Appointment to the order is in the gift of the Queen and is given for personal service to the sovereign. The order is limited to twenty-four, plus the royal knights. Flintshire has two notables who have been, or are, currently members of the order. Throughout the Middle Ages, until the year 1509, ladies could be members of the order, and one of the last during this period was Lady Margaret Beaufort, mother of Henry VII.

In 1987, the right of women to be members of the order was restored and amongst the order was Lady Soames, daughter of former prime minister Winston S. Churchill. Ladies have the initials LG after their name rather than the male, KG. The current member associated with Flintshire, and appointed in 1999, is Sir Erskine William Gladstone, great grandson of the 'grand old man of politics', William Ewart Gladstone. Following war service in the Royal Navy, Sir William graduated from the University of Oxford and pursued a career in teaching, finally retiring as head of Lancing College in 1969, a post he had held since 1961. A committed Boy Scout, he held the post of Chief Scout from 1972 until 1982. In the old county of Clwyd he served as the Queen's personal representative, Lord Lieutenant, from 1985 until 2000.

Another member of the order with local connections is the Duke of Westminster, who was appointed in 2003.

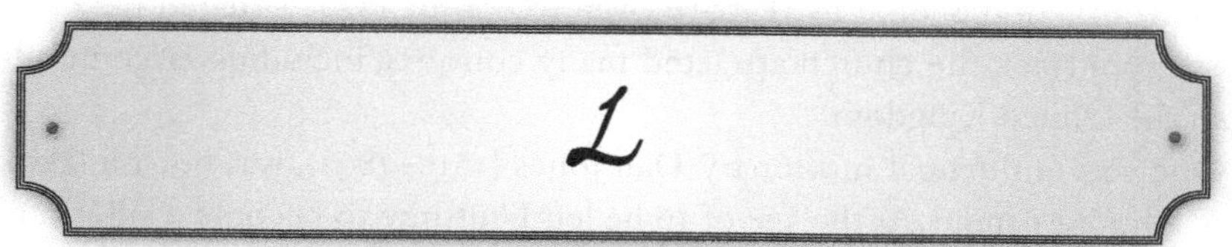

LATTER-DAY SAINTS – HALKYN TO UTAH

At some stage in most people's lives they will have been approached by clean-cut missionaries of the Church of Jesus Christ of Latter-day Saints, better known to most as the Mormons. The church was founded by Joseph Smith in New York State in 1830, and from the outset it encouraged members to become missionaries and bring new people into the church.

The first temple was dedicated at Kirtland in Ohio, but was not popular amongst the established churches, and it is believed that Smith was imprisoned many times for his faith. Due to ongoing persecution, the members moved to

Nauvoo Temple. (Community of Christ Archives, Independence, Mo., USA)

Nauvoo (Hebrew for 'beautiful') in Illinois around 1838–39, and the population grew from 2,900 people in 1840, to over 10,000 in 1844. Situated next to the Mississippi river, the church attracted many converts, including large numbers from the United Kingdom.

One very influential missionary, Dan Jones (1810–1862), was born in Halkyn to Methodist parents. At the age of 16 he left Flintshire to become a sailor, and in 1840 he and his wife, Jane Melling from Denbigh, emigrated to the United States where Jones became captain of steamships on the Mississippi river, and it was during his journeys that he heard of the Mormons' community in Nauvoo. Baptised into the church in 1843, Jones transported converts to Nauvoo as well as materials for the new temple being built in the town.

Following the arrest of Joseph and Hyrum Smith in June 1844, Jones, as a gesture of support, accompanied them to jail. It is said that Joseph Smith made his final prophecy to Jones: 'You will yet see Wales and fulfil the mission appointed you ere you die.' The following day the Smiths were murdered in Carthage Gaol by an armed mob. Jones, meanwhile, had left with a message, and although shot at, he escaped unscathed, if a little frightened.

After the death of Joseph Smith, Brigham Young became the second president of the church, and it was he who led the migration west in 1846–47, leading to the founding of Salt Lake City, Utah. Brigham Young continued with the missionary ethos and, in 1844, Dan Jones travelled back to the United Kingdom and presided over the missionary efforts in Wales, a role he fulfilled for around five years. During this period, he published a Welsh language periodical and pamphlets and these, coupled with his preaching, saw membership of the church increase from approximately 200 in 1844 to over 4,600.

The *Welsh Academy of Wales* states that in 1851 there were twenty Roman Catholic churches in Wales and twenty-eight Mormon places of worship. Accompanied by a large number of converts, Jones returned to America, where a Welsh-speaking branch presided over by Jones was established, and in 1849 he moved with many of these Welsh immigrants to Salt Lake City. Three years later he was requested by Brigham Young to carry out a second mission to Wales and, over the period 1852–56, he carried out successful missionary work with many of the converts eventually emigrating to Utah.

During his stay in Wales, he also translated into Welsh the *Book of Mormon*, which Mormons believe is the scripture handed down to the founder of the church, Joseph Smith. Local converts ignored the dire warnings from other more established religions 'that they would be sold into slavery'. One such convert was John Bennion, who was born in the parish of Hawarden and his story, and those of his descendants, can be found on the website, www.bennion.org.

Dan Jones died on 3 January 1862 and is described by his church as 'one of the most successful and widely known of Latter-day Saints missionaries to the British Isles.'

⁜ LOVE ON/IN THE ROCKS ⁜

The nineteenth-century American journalist and satirist Ambrose Bierce, in his book *The Enlarged Devil's Dictionary*, defines 'love' as 'temporary insanity curable by marriage or by removal of the patient from the influences under which he incurred the disorder'.

In the next couple of stories marriages *did* take place, and the parties expressed their feelings towards each other in very visible fashions.

Following the marriage of Louisa Pennant and Rudolph Viscount Feilding on 18 June 1846, they resolved to build a church to celebrate their marriage (the outcome of which is featured later in the book), and to carry out remodelling to Louisa's ancestral home, Downing Hall. In the 1856 modifications, carried out by T.H. Wyatt, their joint coat of arms and the initials F and P were built into the stonework of the new portico and placed above the first floor window. Sadly, Downing Hall was demolished in 1953–54, but the love token stonework was saved and can be found at Ysgol Bryn Pennant, Mostyn.

The second story relates to a fine late sixteenth or early seventeenth-century house, Fferm. The Grade II listed house, barn and brew house (formerly believed to be the bailiff's cottage) can be found off the Mold–Wrexham road adjacent to Pontblyddyn Cricket Club and forms part of the Hartsheath estate. This wonderful stone-built two-storied manor house, with attics, has retained many of its original features and contains some architectural mysteries.

Love in the stonework. (Rowland Tennant)

Love on the rocks. (Eric Keen)

Originally built on an E-Plan, it was subsequently reduced sometime in the late 1700s, but it does retain two, almost complete, walled gardens believed to be contemporary with the building of the house. The porch, with a date of 1506, is a later addition and is believed to have been brought from another of the owner's properties at Llanfair Dyffryn Clwyd. The love story related to Fferm is that the intertwined initials on the cobbled path are believed to be a commemoration of the marriage, in 1642, of Rhys Lloyd of Fferm and Margaret Ellis of Althrey. Currently covered in moss and grass, it is hoped that these can once again be exposed to the light, although we would not want to be accused of walking through anyone's marriage!

LUFTWAFFE AND THE MOLD ALUN SCHOOLBOY

As we have identified in the decoy site story, Flintshire saw its fair share of Second World War air battles as the county contained a number of industrial and military sites as potential targets. However, many of the German planes seen over Flintshire were en route to the shipyards and other industrial targets on Merseyside.

On 29 May 1941 a Bristol Beaufighter of 604 Squadron, piloted by Squadron Leader Charles Appleton (later Wing Commander), shot down an Orleans-based German Heinkel III, flying at 12,000ft towards its target in Liverpool.

The plane and its bombs were scattered across various locations throughout the area, including the Trap Field in Buckley, where the plane narrowly missed some terraced houses. The crew of four – Lieutenant Helmut Einecke, the pilot; Hans-Georg Hartig, the navigator; Konrad Baron, the mechanic/gunner; and Hans Mulhahn, the wireless operator/gunner – all parachuted safely to earth.

Einecke, who suffered leg injuries on landing, came down in a wooded area near the village of Rhes-y-Cae on Halkyn Mountain. Greeting two startled forestry workers in perfect English, he then asked whether he was near Mold, and whether the Alun School was still there. After receiving confirmation from the forestry workers, he went on to explain the reason for his question. In the pre-war years his family had lived in Flint and he had attended the Alun School before going on to a college in Liverpool in 1938. With the imminent outbreak of war, his family returned to Germany where he enlisted in the Luftwaffe. For the remaining years of the war, he and fellow prisoners of war were employed in forestry work for the Forestry Commission at Wynnstay. Pieces of the destroyed bomber remain, and are held by Flintshire Museum Services.

M

MEDALS FOR COMMEMORATION

We normally associate the award of medals in conjunction with military gallantry, or the Queen's birthday and New Year's Honours lists, but in past centuries these were often given to commemorate some significant local or national event. In September 1888, all the juveniles in the Holywell Workhouse were presented with a medal to commemorate Queen Victoria's visit to Wales, on the occasion of her Golden Jubilee.

Medals were produced with an impression of the Queen on one side and a picture of the monument on Moel Fammau on the reverse. In Halkyn, a house-to-house collection was made to finance the celebrations, with any surplus going towards the proposed library in the village hall. Local people were treated to a tea; there was a procession through the village led by Halkyn Brass Band, followed by sports and other social activities, with a large bonfire and fireworks display to complete the celebrations. The oldest woman in the area was given a shawl and the oldest man a flannel shirt, whilst the children all received medals. What happened to these medals, and do any still exist?

One medal that has survived, celebrating another event, was found by accident in a garden on Halkyn Mountain. This commemorates the first marriage on 16 February 1901, at St Paul's church, Knightsbridge, of 21-year-old Hugh Richard Arthur Grosvenor, 2nd Duke of Westminster, to Constance Edwina (also known as the beautiful 'Shelagh'), a daughter of Colonel Cornwallis-West, of Ruthin Castle. The duke was generally better known to his family by the nickname 'Bendor'. The nickname was given to him by his grandfather, the 1st Duke, as he reminded him of his favourite Derby winner, which also had

Love token. (Sylvia Jones-Davies)

chestnut hair. The medal was presented to the children in the Halkyn/Rhosesmor area who were also treated to a tea party at the Grosvenor-owned Halkyn Castle. Sadly the marriage did not last and they were divorced in 1919, the duke going on to have a further three marriages. This, to the best of our knowledge, is the only surviving coin, unless of course you know better!

Incidentally, the name Bendor continues in the family, as at the time of writing Bendor Grosvenor is listed as an art historian at the Philip Mould Gallery in Mayfair.

The 2nd Duke (1879–1953) served with distinction in the Boer War, and in the First World War, when he was recommended for a Victoria Cross but was subsequently awarded a DSO. A close friend of Winston Churchill, he remained a member of the Conservative party throughout his life, although in the 1930s he supported various right-wing and anti-Semitic causes. A keen sportsman and sailor, he represented Great Britain in motor boat racing at the 1908 London Olympic Games. His many affairs are well documented, including the one lasting ten years with the designer Coco Chanel. However, that was all in the future.

MEDICAL CARE OR POT LUCK?

We are all familiar with 'old wives' tales', particularly on how to deal with medical complaints. Amongst the remedies for headaches is 'rub cow dung and molasses on your temples'; 'tie a buzzard's head around your neck' and (hopefully you have selected a tree with a wide girth if you use this particular method) 'lean your head against a tree and have someone else drive a nail into the opposite side of the tree'.

The Egyptians had an advanced medical system, and the Romans spread their medical expertise throughout the Empire. Following the departure of the Romans from Britain, medical treatment for the poor was generally provided by religious establishments. In Flintshire it is likely that Basingwerk Abbey, at Greenfield, would have catered for the needs of the sick. However, it is also likely that those caring for the sick reverted to 'natural' and folk remedies, with the underlying principle being that of 'humours'.

It was believed that within every individual there were four 'humours', or principal fluids – black bile, yellow bile, phlegm and blood. The four humours were associated with the four seasons – autumn, summer, winter and spring – respectively. These were produced by various organs in the body, and they had to be in balance for a person to remain healthy. Too much phlegm in the body, for example, caused lung problems, and the body tried to cough up the phlegm to restore a balance. The balance of humours in humans could be achieved by diet, medicines, and by bloodletting using leeches. This belief persevered well into the nineteenth century.

So, what sort of treatments could we expect to receive in our county? Many of the cures put forward involved 'wise women' who, having eaten different types of birds could, by breathing down the patient's throat, cure them of particular illnesses. The following are taken from a paper written by A.D. Carr, entitled 'Some Seventeenth-Century Remedies' and published in Volume 24 of the *Journal of the Flintshire Historical Society*:

> A medicine to kyll the wormes
> Of Alasacatrine [fir tree resin] Steeped overnyght in the Joyce [juice] of wormwood spred upon ij peece of lether thone most be layed upon the stomake thother upon the navell 3 howres after, both most be left till they fall of themselves.
>
> A medicine approved for the Gowt
> Take two spoonefulls of Rye flower, and one spoonefull of redd lead, with two other spoonefulls of wynne vynegar, and mixt all this, and make of it a plaster after laie it upon a cleane cloth, and applie it to the place ill affected, as ofte as it is dried, take a newe plaster, and applie it untill the paine be gone.
>
> To break the wyndiness of the stomacke
> Take comyn seed, fenell seede and annys seede of each like quantity, beate them to a powder and boyle the same well in whitt or clarett wyne, and drinke a good draught thearof warme morninge and evening for 5 or 6 dayes together and you shall find ease thearby.
>
> For the Paulsey
> Brewe good store of rosmary & redsage in your drinkee, & drinke of it continually with the powder of red sage as much as you can, and eate the powder of sage with your meate in steade of salte. Boyle mustard & vineger together in a pipkin & caste a sheete over your heade and winke with your eyes & receave the fume of it as hote as you can holdinge your mouth open over it, doe soe at night when you goe to bed & in the morninge foure or five daies before you anoynte you. Use to Chawe tobacco in your mouth & swallow the Joyce [juice] of it & keepe the tobacco in your mouth till it make you cast, doe soe once in to or three daies tell you ffinde your palsey to mend. Anonynte all your numed partes with horse grece before a fier every night & morninge, a whole houre together & after your oyntinge in the morninge goe to bed & cover you very warme & sweate if you can one houre.

Whilst I recognise that these various remedies sound very tempting, please do not try them at home!

Locally, Thomas Griffiths of Rhual graduated in 1725 as a doctor of medicine awarded by the Academy of Leyden, Netherlands (whose alumni include Albert Einstein), and as well as being a close friend of Sir George Wynne of

Leeswood Hall, he also acted as his medical adviser. Sadly we do not have details of what sort of remedies he used.

The Methodist founder, John Wesley, had *Primitive Physic* published in 1747, and this contained many suggested remedies for common complaints. For a hoarse voice he recommended the following: 'Rub the soles of the feet, in front of the fire, with garlic and lard, well beaten together'; and for gout:

> At six in the evening undress and wrap yourself up in blankets, then put your legs up to the knees in water, as hot as you can bear it. As it cools, let hot water be poured in so as to keep you in a strong sweat till ten. Then go into a bed well warmed and sweat till morning.

Whether Wesley used these 'cures' on his visits to Flintshire we will never know.

To complete this section I combed a collection of folklore and anthropology listed with the title *100 Ways to Avoid Dying*, and I leave the reader with the following thought: 'When sick, don't look in mirrors.'

MUSIC AND MENDELSSOHN'S LOGGERHEADS COMPOSITION

The house called Coed Du on the outskirts of Rhydymwyn was once rented by John Taylor, the Cornish mining engineer who was employed by the Grosvenor estate. During his stay Taylor, or rather his daughters, were visited in 1829 by the famous German composer Felix Mendelssohn who, whilst in the area, wrote three pieces of music – 'Andante and Allegro in A minor', 'Capriccio in E minor', and 'Andante in E Major' (The Rivulet). A letter, written by Mendelssohn on 2 September 1829, describes them as 'three of my best piano compositions' and goes into the background of their inspiration:

> For the two younger sisters I took the carnations and roses and began to write music. And for the other sister I composed the 'Rivulet' which has pleased us so much during our ride that we dismounted and sat down by it … I believe it is the best I have done in that way; it is so flowing and quiet, and drowsily simple, that I have played it to myself every day …

Mendelssohn also wrote the music for a number of hymns, including 'Hark the Herald Angels Sing', 'Hear My Prayer' (with the rousing verse 'On the wings of a dove …') and 'Hymn of Praise' (1840). The last of these was called, by the family, the 'Printers' Cantata' and appropriately was commissioned to celebrate the four hundredth anniversary of Gutenberg's moveable-type printing press.

However, Mendelssohn was less than impressed with Welsh music, as indicated by a letter written from an inn in Llangollen:

> Ten thousand devils take all national music! Here I am in Wales, and, heaven help us! A harper sits in the hall of every reputable tavern incessantly playing the so-called folk melodies – that is to say, dreadful, vulgar, out-of-tune trash with a hurdy-gurdy going at the same time! It has given me toothache already.

Clearly he may have changed his opinion in the twenty-first century, when a capacity crowd at the Millennium Stadium spontaneously broke out into Max Boyce's 'Hymns and Arias' after Wales had just scored a try against England!

The visit by Mendelssohn is recorded by a memorial stone mounted in a wall in Rhydymwyn. This advises that the Reverend Charles Kingsley, the author of *The Water Babies*, also visited the area. From 1870 to 1873, Kingsley was a canon of Chester Cathedral and was a founder member of the Chester Society for Natural Science, Literature & Art. This society was at the forefront of the movement to establish the still popular Chester Grosvenor Museum, and one of his poems 'Sands of the Dee' will feature later in the book.

N

NAPOLEON AND THE LINK WITH LEESWOOD HALL

There are many links connecting Flintshire people with the Napoleonic Wars, including the Morgan family of Golden Grove, near Llanasa, and the heir to the Rhual Estate, Mold, Major Edwin Griffith of the 15th (King's) Hussars, who was killed at the Battle of Waterloo in 1815.

The diaries and journals of Major Griffith and his nephew, Captain Frederick Griffith, are detailed in Gareth Glover's evocative book *From Corunna to Waterloo*. Whilst some of the content is related to domestic matters, they do describe the difficult life for British soldiers during the various campaigns, as well as describing in graphic detail the poverty and suffering of many of the Spanish people caught up in the war.

Mind you, not everyone was at Waterloo through choice, as reported in the Darlington-based *Northern Echo* of 2 March 1896: 'Robert Williams has just died at the Holywell Workhouse. It appears that the deceased, whose father was a soldier, was born at the English camp at Waterloo on the day of the battle, June 15 1815.'

As well as soldiers, there are various links with the Royal Navy, the most notorious being that of Nelson's mistress, Emma Lady Hamilton. Although born in the parish of Neston in Cheshire, the daughter of a blacksmith, she spent her early childhood in Hawarden and, at age 12, she is recorded as working as a maid in the Hawarden home of Dr H.L. Thomas. After a number of years in London, she married Sir William Hamilton, the British Government's representative to the Court of Naples, and it was whilst in Naples that she began her relationship with Admiral Nelson. Following Nelson's death at the Battle of Trafalgar, Emma was shunned by society and died in poverty in Calais in 1815.

The grave of a sailor who served under Nelson at Trafalgar can be found in Bistre churchyard, Buckley. Edward Bellis, aged 88 years, is described on his headstone as 'our Pensioner of Greenwich Hospital, died in 1848 and interred at Bistree'.

Recruitment into the forces was not always optional and the 'Press Gang' was always looking for 'volunteers' to man Royal Navy warships. One centenarian resident of Holywell Workhouse, named Hewitt, could recall the Battle of Trafalgar, and in his words, his 'father being on Nelson's ship, having being carried from his home by a press gang'.

A further link with Nelson is Admiral Thomas Totty, whose family home was Cornist Hall, Flint. He served as the third in command of the Baltic Fleet under Hyde Parker and Nelson.

The last of our links with Nelson is the principal subject of this story. This particular Royal Navy officer met with and was presented with a memento from the hand of the defeated Emperor Napoleon Bonaparte. William Wynne-Eyton of Leeswood Hall joined the navy as a first class volunteer on 10 July 1805. Aged 11 years, he served as midshipman aboard HMS *Neptune*, captained by Thomas F. Freemantle. In October of that year the ship took part in the Battle of Trafalgar, and afterwards was the vessel that towed HMS *Victory* into Gibraltar for repair. Subsequently, William served aboard HMS *Sea Horse*, *Milford* and *Ajax*, and his logbook for 1810–11 records several places where they had anchored, including Cagliari in Sardinia.

Midshipman Wynne-Eyton and 'Boney's' medal. (Charles Wynne-Eyton)

It was an incident whilst he was serving aboard the *Ajax*, on 11 September 1810, which he recalls very vividly in his logbook: 'At 5 a.m. Light airs inclinable to calm. Port Ferajo in the Island of Elba bearing about SE by S, 5 or 6 leagues. A Brig was seen from the poop, East, apparently a Merchantman becalmed'. The decision was made to take this ship, and under his command four boats, including the captain's cutter carrying seven officers and fifty-four sailors and marines, set off. Life was not easy for the ordinary sailors, as the logbook records: 'After a tedious pull of nearly three hours we came within gun shot of the Brig who hoisted French colours and fired a stern chase which went short of us'. Still unsure of what they were dealing with, they pursued their attack and, covered by small arms fire, they prepared to board the vessel until the incoming fire, including grapeshot, got heavier. Faced with heavy fire they used 'what few oars could be managed to go back astern' and William records what they had attempted to board:

> From several officers in cocked hats we now found she was a man-of-war full of men and perfectly prepared for us in every respect, her tops full of small-armed men, swivels on her stern and a regular tier of guns which she had deferred firing until we were alongside.

The brig chose not to pursue them, and on returning to the *Ajax* they found that one officer and five seamen had been killed, and one officer and eleven seamen wounded. Fortunately, William came out physically unscathed with his career intact and the next time we meet him is on the HMS *Bellerophon*, under the command of Captain Maitland. The *Bellerophon*, built by Edward Greaves & Co., of Frindsbury, Kent, was launched in 1786, carried seventy-four guns, weighed 1,612 tons and had a compliment of 550 sailors and marines. The ship saw much action, including the Battles of the Nile and Trafalgar, but it is the events following the Battle of Waterloo that bring her to prominence. Napoleon, attempting to flee France on 15 July 1815, was forced to surrender to Captain Maitland and he remained on the *Bellerophon* until 7 August when he was transferred to HMS *Northumberland* for onward transportation to exile on St Helena.

Whilst on board the *Bellerophon*, whose officers included William Wynne-Eyton, Napoleon was painted by a number of notable artists, including Sir Charles Lock Eastlake and Sir William Quiller Orchardson. However, the artists were not allowed on board, and they sketched from the flotilla of small boats carrying onlookers attempting to get a sight of the deposed emperor. The ship's nickname was 'Billy Ruffian' and a folk song entitled 'Boney was a Warrior' contains a verse highlighting the link with the ship:

> Boney went a-cruisin'
> Way-aye-yah!
> Aboard the Billy Ruffian.

Various memorabilia associated with ship and its crew can be found in a number of public collections, but William Wynne-Eyton, along with the officers of the *Bellerophon*, received a personal gift from Napoleon. They all received a miniature *Légion d'honneur*, and pictured on page 92 is William Wynne-Eyton as a midshipman, along with this medal.

William remained in the navy and rose to the rank of captain. In 1855 we find him, along with fellow officers, attending the jubilee celebrations of the Battle of Trafalgar. He died at Leeswood Hall on 6 June 1857, and a window depicting the 'Stilling of the Storm' in the north side of the chancel of Pontblyddyn church is dedicated to his memory. As for the *Bellerophon*, her life as a ship of the line was over, and in 1815 she was converted into a prison ship, renamed very appropriately *Captivity*, before finally being scrapped in 1836.

ODDS AND ENDS

Bagillt and Patagonia

The settlement of the Welsh in Patagonia in the nineteenth century is an established fact, but the legacy from the emigration of Bagillt citizens is perhaps not so well known. On the edge of a lake in the Andes, near the town of Trevelin, will be found the town of Llyn Bagillt. The area also boasts a nature reserve, some 30km (19 miles) from Trevelin in Cwm Hyfryd, which is called Lago Bagillt.

One passenger on the Patagonia-bound vessel *Mimosa* in 1865 was the 20-year-old Denbigh-born Joseph Seth Jones, and he kept a diary in which he recorded all the trials and tribulations of the first Welsh settlers in Patagonia. In 1866, he subsequently travelled to the Falkland Islands, before returning to Wales in May 1868. On his return he lived in Holywell and worked for the post office, on the Bagillt round, until his retirement in August 1904. He died in January 1912, and reports state that his funeral was attended by hundreds of mourners. Reflecting his religious and community involvement, the mourners included twenty ministers of religion of various denominations.

BBC and the Bruised Ego!

A number of years ago, the author was involved with BBC Wales in the making of a programme called *Jamie and Derek's Welsh Weekends*, featuring the television newsreader and broadcaster Jamie Owen and BBC weatherman Derek Brockway. The filming, in Mold town centre, was carried out on a cold May Bank Holiday Saturday morning, whilst the crowded street market was in full swing. As may be expected, the presence of two well-known figures attracted a lot of attention and, during a break in filming, we were approached by a lady keen to meet television personalities. She, first of all, told Jamie that she always watched the BBC Wales news, and his wonderful travel programmes, then turned to Derek and made similar comments about watching the weather and his programme *The Weatherman Walking*. After singing their praises for some time she turned to the author, standing between the two stars, and remarked, 'Should I know you?' – So much for fame!

Who are you? (Eric Keen)

Copper Bottoms and Trafalgar

Greenfield Valley has long been recognised as being at the forefront of the industrial development of Flintshire, but it also played an important role in a major sea battle. Thomas Williams, the 'Copper King', founded the Parys Mine Company on Anglesey in 1774. The ore was then taken to his works at Swansea (nicknamed 'Copperopolis') or St Helens, where it was smelted. Copper ingots were shipped to the Greenfield works where a variety of products were manufactured, including items associated with the slave trade.

At this time, Royal Naval vessels were made of wood, making their hulls susceptible to damage, and ultimate destruction, from the Teredo Navalis worm. Williams' works at Greenfield produced bolts to a secret formula, and also copper sheets which were fitted to the hulls of British ships, including HMS *Victory*. Not only did the sheets protect the ships' hulls, but it made them faster and more manoeuvrable, thereby giving Nelson and his Royal Navy a considerable advantage at the Battle of Trafalgar.

When the copper sheets were eventually removed from HMS *Victory*, two of them were purchased by the local authority and can now be seen at the Greenfield Heritage Park museum.

Eyes Front

For those who watch the great ceremonial and commemoration events and wonder who planned and organised the often complicated routines, well, for the past decade, that accolade belongs to a soldier born on Deeside.

Garrison Sergeant Major Bill Mott is the Senior Warrant Officer in the British Army, and the design of his badge of rank is personally approved by the sovereign. He originally enlisted in the 1st Battalion of the Royal Welch Fusiliers and his service included operational tours to Northern Ireland, the 1982 retaking of the Falkland Islands, and he also served as an instructor at the Royal Military Academy, Sandhurst. Fly into Terminal 5 at Heathrow Airport and you will be greeted by his image on a 30ft poster, and if you are considering buying a particular military action figure, you will discover Bill Mott's voice barking out the orders. He continues a family tradition, as two of his brothers are also military men.

'God Save the King' comes to Moel Fammau

Throughout the years, many people will have walked to the summit of Moel Fammau and enjoyed the extensive views from the remains of the Jubilee Tower, the foundation stone of which was laid by Lord Kenyon on 25 October 1810. The cost of the tower, commemorating the jubilee of George III, was raised by public subscription.

At the opening, the large crowd was regaled with numerous speeches and poems, before tucking into a nineteenth-century barbeque – an ox roast. As was normal on such occasions, the event was brought to an end by the singing of the British national anthem ('*Hen Wlad fy Nhadau*' or 'Land of My Fathers' was not composed until the mid-1850s), for which additional stanzas were composed. The last stanza was as follows:

And as this joyous day
The Grateful Pile we lay
To Britain's King;
By love, by freedom led,
We'll rear its towering head,
Firm as its rocky bed,
To George our King.

Sadly for the tower, the upper portion of the 115ft-high structure wasn't as firm as was hoped and it was blown down during a severe gale on 1 November 1862.

Hartsheath Hall and Charles Dickens Jnr

Mold's very own gifted writer, politician, preacher and tailor, Daniel Owen, is often referred to, rightly or wrongly, as the 'Dickens of Wales'. Much of his writing has been considered autobiographical, and people, places and events can

Architect, actor or spendthrift? (David Rowe)

be identified from his various novels. Unlike Charles Dickens, Daniel does not appear to have been credited with publishing biographies.

In the early nineteenth century Hartsheath Hall, Pontblyddyn, came into the possession of the Welsh Mining Company and they engaged a Liverpool-born architect, Charles James Mathews (1803–1878), to adapt the building to form a residence for the company's director. Mathews served an apprenticeship under the renowned architect Augustus Charles Pugin, and followed this profession for a number of years. The company set a budget of £2,500 for the work, but the actual expenditure amounted to some £5,000, and it is believed that as a result of this large financial outlay, the company went out of business.

The house was sold to the Jones family in 1829, and their descendants remain in occupation today. As for Mathews, he eventually left the profession and became a very successful actor, starring in light comedy roles in London, France and the United States. His fame was recognised by Charles Dickens' son, who wrote *The Life of Charles Mathews*, comprising two volumes. In the book, Dickens Junior uses Mathews' own writings to record the period, between 1824 and 1826, when he was resident in Wales: 'For more than a year my headquarters were held at a quaint old Welsh farm at Pontblyddyn, about half a mile across the meadows from Heartsheath …' The quaint farmhouse is believed to be Fferm, which features in an earlier story.

Home from Home?

Oliver Twist by Charles Dickens paints a grim picture of life in workhouses and, in Holywell, many of the original workhouse buildings can still be seen.

Not everyone saw these as bleak establishments. In 1880, Holywell Workhouse was described as 'one of the most delightfully situated "Hotels" in the Kingdom … it looks from a distance like the residence of some opulent gentleman, who have lived honest, hard working lives'. It's not clear whether the residents of the workhouse would feel the same. This, despite the fact that some Guardians were expressing concern that it cost 1*s* 10*d* a week to keep someone in Holywell, whilst the St Asaph Union only spent 1*s* 7*d* per week. Mind you, questions were asked in 1886 when it was disclosed that Chester Workhouse, with 675 inmates, only spent £8 on supplying 'stimulants' to sick inmates, whereas Holywell spent £14 on its 225 inmates. The Holywell Union chairman, addressing the workhouse doctor, said that he trusted him to use stimulants only when necessary, but went on to suggest that he use milk instead!

Past their Sell By Date?

In the County Museum store will be found an interesting donation to the various collections – a bottle of preserved plums, bottled on 11 August 1945 by Mrs Gladys Morgan of Shotton. Would you want to try them?

Pint or Filling, Sir? But Mind the Cattle!

The visit to the dentist is one many of us make with some trepidation, but when the dentist starts to appear in the local hostelry, many people will consider this a step, or indeed a filling, too far. A Mold dentist, M.B. Thompson of Clifton House, Wrexham Street, advertised with slogans such as 'Positively Painless Extractions' and 'Teeth without a plate a Speciality'. He also practised his profession at the Royal Oak, Halkyn, so after recovering from the gas, or perhaps a tot of whisky after a 'painless extraction', you may have thought you were still dazed when you read the following report of Mold licensing sessions held in September 1896:

> Mr Bernard Lewis yesterday, at the adjourned Mold Licensing Session, applied on behalf of James Evans, for the revival of an off-beerhouse license for a place known as the 'Shop' Bryn-y-Baal, Mold. He stated that since the application was first made he had been supplied with important information regarding the claims of the house. It was situated in an agricultural district, and was a great convenience to the farmers to get beer for their cattle in time of sickness. Previously he had been of the opinion that cattle were teetotallers. (Laughter.) – The Chairman: 'Is this the first time you have heard that cattle take beer?' – Mr Lewis: 'Yes, it is.' – Two farmers gave evidence in favour of the application. However, the Bench was not swayed and refused the licence.

Rolls-Royce Lovers

Many of us like executive luxury cars and perhaps even dream of owning a Rolls-Royce. For Frank, a former Rolls-Royce employee, and Audrey Russell, of Rhes-y-Cae, their lifelong passion and love for this particular car was carried to their joint grave. Mrs Russell, whose husband predeceased her by three months, left instructions with her solicitors regarding the type of headstone required. She requested a headstone in the shape of a Rolls-Royce grille, and the pictured memorial, carved in India, can be found in Rhes-y-Cae churchyard.

The Russells' headstone. (David Rowe)

Smallest Colliery Workers
Born into a family of little people, James and John Smith of Buckley were employed at the Buckley Mountain Colliery, where they were responsible for the miners' lamps. It is claimed they were the smallest colliery workers in Great Britain, as James was 36in in height and John, who stood on a table to carry out his work, only measured 30in. Along with their sister, Mary, they were believed to be excellent singers and often performed as a trio in local entertainment shows. John was born in 1859 and James in 1861 and they both lived on into their 70s.

What's in a Name?
During the nineteenth century, the county saw the influx of many *Sais* coming to work in the extensive mining, quarrying, brickmaking and pottery industries, and often changing predominately Welsh-speaking areas forever. This was particularly true in the Pontblyddyn, Coed Talon, Treuddyn, Leeswood and Nercwys areas, where many English coal miners appear to have settled. This immigration was, as you can imagine, not universally popular with the local miners and, irrespective of their county of origin, these incomers were called 'Lancys' (Lancastrians) and derogatory poems were even written about them. In some cases, local miners' families were evicted from their homes to accommodate the incomers. In the case of Nercwys, one row of terraced houses, near Church View, is still called 'Lancys Row'.

Will These Last?
Casual conversations, overheard on local transport, often result in the listener discovering the most intimate medical details, but it was a more mundane, if not touching, matter exercising a gentleman on a bus travelling from an outlying village into Mold. The discussion was related to the purchase of a new pair of shoes, with the purchaser wondering which shop to visit. Concerned about the lasting quality of the new purchase, he decided in the end to go to the Clark's shop, as 'you know they will last'. Admirable sentiment you may agree, particularly as the purchaser was only 107 years old!

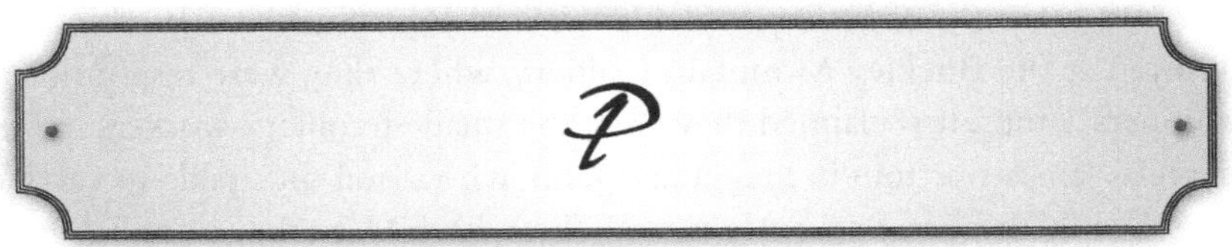

POETS

Bagillt has been the birthplace of a number of notable men, often born into poverty but who made a success of their lives. One such man was Enoch Robert Salisbury (1819–1890), MP and lawyer, and we will hear more of him later in the book.

Amongst the mining fraternity was George Tattum (1870–1941) who worked at the nearby Bettisfield Colliery and became known as 'The Miners' Welsh Poet.' Described as the son of a chemical labourer, he was self-taught, and his poems reflected all aspects of life in the tightly knit Bagillt community.

In addition to local poets, the area was associated with two incomers whose poetry and lives were very different, although it is quite possible that they knew each other. The Jesuit priest, Gerald Manley Hopkins (1844–1889), who we heard of earlier, studied theology at St Beuno's College, Tremeirchion. The majority of Hopkins' work was not published during his lifetime but, as is often the case, after his death its true quality was realised and appreciated.

The presence of the religious establishments of St Beuno's College and St David's Friary, Pantasaph, attracted many people, some of whom were troubled personalities. The next poet certainly falls into that category. Described variously as 'The Poet of Catholicism' or the 'Pantasaph Poet', the Preston-born Francis Thompson (1859–1907) was educated at Ushaw College Catholic Seminary in Durham, and then studied medicine at Owens College, Manchester. However, unlike his father, Thompson did not end up practicing medicine, because he saw his future in writing.

In 1885, he moved to London with the sole aim of becoming a writer but without any independent means of support, so he ended up living rough on the streets. He subsequently applied for admission to Oxford University, but by then he had become addicted to opium so his application was rejected.

We next find him at Pantasaph, where he is recorded in 1892 as living with a family called Brien at the friary-owned Bishop's House. He appears to have enjoyed a good relationship with the friars, and particularly Father Anselm (who went on to become Archbishop of Simla – formerly the summer capital of British India), who visited Thompson every other day. Contemporary sources also detail Thompson's visits to St Beuno's College and his pilgrimage to St Winefride's Well. When the Briens moved to another friary-owned house called Crecas Cottage, Thompson initially remained at Bishop's House. However, after a row with his new landlady, he had a short stay at the nearby Ivy Cottage before rejoining the Briens still living in small Crecas Cottage.

During his time at Pantasaph, he enjoyed a close relationship with the unmarried Maggie Brien, but although they appear to have cared deeply for each other, the relationship eventually came to naught. It was during Thompson's time at Pantasaph that his friends, Wilfred and Alice Meynall, recognised the quality of his poetry and arranged with a publisher, John Lane, to publish his work. Thompson left the area in 1896, but continued his successful and paying writing career until his death in London on 13 November 1907. He is buried in St Mary's Roman Catholic cemetery, Kensal Green, in London.

The following extract from a poem written for children, 'Ex Ore Infantium' is one of many poems written by Thompson and perhaps reflects his very troubled character:

> Little Jesus, wast Thou shy
> Once, and just so small as I?
> And what did it feel like to be
> Out of Heaven, and just like me?
> Didst Thou sometimes think of THERE,
> And ask where all the angels were?
> I should think that I would cry
> For my house all made of sky;
> I would look about the air,
> And wonder where my angels were;
> And at waking 'twould distress me–
> Not an angel there to dress me!
> Hadst thou ever any toys,
> Like us little girls and boys?
> And didst Thou play in Heaven with all
> The angels that were not too tall
> With the stars for marbles.

G.K. Chesterton said of Thompson after his death: 'with Francis Thompson we lost the greatest poetic energy since Browning.' The *Penny Illustrated Paper* of 25 November 1911, summed up his life and legacy:

> Since his death three or four years ago Thompson's poems have sold to the tune of thirty to forty thousand copies; that he has been acclaimed amongst the great English poets … a movement is afoot to place a memorial to him in Westminster Abbey; whereas during his lifetime Thompson starved, begged and slept on the embankment …

Unfortunately Thompson did not make it into Poet's Corner but his legacy lives on in his extensive poetry, and eighty-seven of these can be found on the website www.poemhunter.com/francis-thompson/poems.

PANTASAPH AND PUGIN, OR TWO ANGLICANS = ONE CATHOLIC

In the previous story we were introduced by Francis Thompson to the Capuchin friars at St David's, Pantasaph, and the story of how they arrived in the area and established the friary is possibly well known to many readers. The site of the friary was on land owned by Louisa Pennant of nearby Downing and, as previously mentioned, she married Rudolph, Viscount Feilding (later the 8th Earl of Denbigh) on 18 June 1846. Devoted to each other, as committed Anglicans they agreed to build an Anglican church in celebration of their marriage, and the architect James Wyatt was employed to design and supervise the work.

Whilst construction was underway, the couple travelled to Europe, including Rome, where they were granted an audience with Pope Pius IX, and this sowed the seeds of their ultimate conversion. When, in 1850, Louisa fell sick and her condition worsened whilst undergoing treatment in Edinburgh, they made the decision to convert to Catholicism. Therefore, on their return to Downing they felt that the church they had commissioned, at a personal cost of some £10,000 or more, could no longer be handed over to the Anglican Church and the building would instead be given to the Catholic Church.

This decision provoked a storm of protest. Effigies of Viscount Feilding were burnt in Holywell and Mostyn, lengthy and acrimonious correspondence was exchanged with the Bishop of St Asaph, and even Feilding's own father temporarily disinherited him. Litigation followed, but the courts upheld their right to gift the property to the Catholic Church. Following their conversion, the Feildings spent a considerable period of time in Italy, where they made the acquaintance of the Capuchin Franciscan friars and subsequently they gifted Pantasaph, with other endowments, to the order which remains in residence today.

In response, the Anglican Church decided to launch an appeal for funds to build a church to replace the one at Pantasaph. However, it was also decided that one church was insufficient to meet the 'spiritual wants' of the local population, so new churches were erected at Gorsedd and Brynford instead. Donations, in varying amounts, flooded in from across the country, with the highest being £500 from a Mrs Pennant; £200 from the Dowager Duchess of Devonshire; £150 from the Earl of Cardigan; and £100 each from the Bishop of St Asaph, the Dean of St Asaph, Marquis of Westminster, Earl Howe, Lord Dinorben, the Misses Luxmoore of Bryn Asaph, John Day Senior of Tottenham, Hon. Colonel Douglas

Pennant, Major Ingleby of Panton Hall, Mrs Park of Ince Hall, Chester, Reverend J.E. Cross of Appleby, the Duke of Cleveland and Messrs Newton, Keates & Co.

In the meantime James Wyatt, who had built St David's in a neo-Gothic style, did not wish to continue working on a Catholic church, and an architect to adapt the building for Catholic worship was required. The leading architect of the time was August Welby Pugin (1812–1852), who himself had converted to Catholicism in 1835, and he had gained his reputation from various projects including the Houses of Parliament (in conjunction with Charles Barry), St George's Cathedral, Southwark, and Alton Towers.

He also wrote a number of architectural books including *Gothic Furniture in the Style of the Fifteenth Century*, *The True Principles of Pointed or Christian Architecture*, *An Apology for the Revival of Christian Architecture in London*, and *A Treatise on Chancel Screens and Rood Lofts*. His national importance was recognised when he was appointed Commissioner of Fine Arts for 'The Great Exhibition of the Industry of all Nations', held in the Crystal Palace from 6 September to 11 October 1851. The total number of visitors was 6,063,986, with the largest attendance on one day (7 October) recorded as 93,224. The cost of day admission was 2*s* 6*d*, and the total sum raised over the life of the event was £505,117 5*s* 6*d*.

Pugin's Pantasaph reredos. (David Rowe)

Viscount Feilding amidst the Pugin Gothic. (Peter Robinson)

Pugin exhibited at the event's 'A Medieval Court', and it is said that Queen Victoria made a special visit to look at some of his work. Several items of Pugin's work displayed at the Great Exhibition were purchased by Viscount Feilding, and brought to Pantasaph where they remain today. These items were designed by Pugin, but are likely to have been produced by his two craftsmen, George Myers and John Hardman. Among the Pugin treasures at Pantasaph are the pictured reredos in the Lady Chapel, a statue of Madonna and Child, the great cross and the high altar. The remainder of the church was decorated in the unique Pugin gothic design, and the church was dedicated to St David with St Asaph as a secondary patron, and opened on 13 October 1852.

The decoration, or indeed Catholicism, was not to everyone's taste, as reflected in an article in the *North Wales Chronicle* of 7 August, 1858: 'and few can fail to regard with wonder the extraordinary fact, that such puerile fancies and superstitious legends should form, in the nineteenth century and in the heart of Protestant Britain ...'

Sadly, Louisa did not have the opportunity to enjoy worship in their newly endowed church, as she died in Naples on 3 May 1853. Her body was returned to her beloved Pantasaph and interred in the family vault. Rudolph remarried in 1857 and, whilst living at Downing, he and his new wife joined the Third Order of St Francis. Viscount Feilding and his second wife continued to live charitable lives, and they were known for their religious adherence as well as their daily support of the poor and sick. Feilding died at Newnham Paddox on 10 March 1892, and his body was brought by rail to Holywell station, from where it was carried by the friars to Pantasaph and placed in the vault next to his first wife. Even in death his link with the Third Order of St Francis is reflected, as the statue, depicting a recumbent Viscount Feilding, is attired in the robes of the order.

POLITICS – FLOWERS AND VERMIN

Whilst many people in the twenty-first century steer clear of politics in all its forms, this is not a new phenomenon, and political parties have always sought ways to encourage voters to cast their vote in their favour. So, when the *Cheshire Observer* of 29 December 1888 announced that a Grand Character Concert for the Primrose League was to be held at the Foundry, Hawarden, the question was asked: what was this organisation named after a flower?

The event was to be chaired by Thomas Bate, of the Kelsterton Brewery, with the purpose of inaugurating the 'Mostyn-Hawarden Habitation of the Primrose League'. Tickets were available from various locations, including the Fox Inn, Hawarden. Throughout the centuries, political parties of all colours have always attempted to influence voters to support their particular candidate. This could have been by means of direct bribery, threats of violence, or dismissal from your job and home, or even promises of a 'Utopia' that we could all enjoy in the future. The Conservative party had two organisations to assist with their efforts to get enough voters to allow them to form a government.

Primrose League badge. (John King)

The *Wrexham Advertiser* of 30 November 1883 reports on the Primrose League with a little touch of sarcasm:

> Colours seem to be rapidly coming into fashion as a mark of brotherhood in any particular society. The Salvation Army has given us the red, the Cerulean Army the blue, and now we are to have the yellow of the Primrose League. A news paragraph in a morning contemporary says that a Primrose League has been formed with a view to carrying out a certain political programme. This is all very well. Doubtless the arrangement is very straightforward and very good, but where are we to stop? Why not have the Rose Society for admitting women to the franchise; the Wallflower Band for securing a repeal of the prohibitions on deceased wives' sisters; the Geranium Fraternity, for abolishing Billingsgate; the Dahlia Brotherhood, to bring about vegetarianism; the Dandelion, for promoting municipal reform; the Pansy Society, for repealing the Contagious Diseases Act; or the Rhododendron Lads sworn to spoil pigeon shooting? A member of one or two of these might have the emblems worked on his coat would look very pretty.

The Primrose League was formed at the Carlton Club, London, in late 1883 and amongst its founder members was Winston Churchill's father, Lord Randolph Churchill. Its declared aim was to rectify 'the failure of Conservative and Constitutional Associations to suit the popular taste or to succeed in joining all classes together for political objects'.

Membership was declared as being open to all, including Catholics, and even women from 1885, although atheists and enemies of the British Empire were excluded. It is claimed that it was named after Disraeli's favourite flower, the variety Queen Victoria sent him on more than one occasion, including to his funeral. It may still be the case that the flowers are laid at the foot of his statues each year – when the author visited Disraeli's home at Hughenden Manor, in April 2013, it coincided with the anniversary of Disraeli's death and a bunch of primroses and a small display were laid out for visitors.

The activities of the league, and particularly the ladies, were widely reported in the local press, although this was not often sympathetically. Typical of the comments is the following, reported in the *Wrexham Advertiser* on 7 November 1885:

> I hear the gentler sex of the members of the League are the chief workers. The present duties of these ladies it appears is to visit the wives of working men voters, while their husbands are at work, and endeavour to instil in their minds the idea that should their husbands vote for a Liberal candidate, it will be the cause of the old Church of England being swept from the face of the earth …

Or that published on 5 November 1887:

> One of the Lady Presidents [of the Primrose League] was one day listening to her little boy saying his prayers, and he prayed, as children did, for the King and Queen, and all his friends, and all the great people he had heard. At last he turned to his mother and asked if he should pray for the Prime Minister [Conservative – Liberal Coalition], and the mother wishing to reconcile her Christian Charity, with her political principles, at last said 'Pray that he may become a Conservative …'

Despite the vitriol from many newspapers, the organisation grew rapidly throughout the years – from 957 members in 1884 to over 2 million in 1910 – and it continued to fight elections until at least the 1930s. Members were called 'Knights', 'Dames' or 'Associates', and local groups were known as 'Habitations', of which there were over 2,600 at its peak.

A trawl of local newspapers turns up the league's activities in Flintshire, under the overall name of the Mostyn Habitation. The *Wrexham Advertiser* of 21 November 1885 informs us of the formation of a branch of the Primrose League in Mold:

> On Friday evening a meeting was held at the Stores, Church Lane, to inaugurate the formation of a branch or habitation of the Primrose League. The meeting was numerously attended. Lord Mostyn presided, and a number of ladies occupied seats upon the platform.
>
> His Lordship having read the proposed bye-laws of the Mold Branch of Mostyn Habitation, introduced Mr Wilson Fox, London, who delivered an amusing speech, in the course of which he explained the object of the League, viz., 'the dissemination and upholding of Constitutional principles as opposed to the Radicalism of the present day, which threatened to destroy the institution which had conduced to the glory and welfare of the empire.' He referred to the extension of the League, branches of it having been formed not only in the United Kingdom but also in the Indian Empire.
>
> As to the local branch, thanks to the energy and zeal of Miss Raikes, Llwynegryn, the Hon. Secretary of the Habitation, 200 names had already been enrolled, and he expressed the hope that at the close of this meeting that number would be considerably augmented.

Further branches could be found at other locations within Flintshire, including Hawarden, Holywell, Flint, Caerwys, Hope and Caergwrle.

The three main areas of local concern for the league were the drive for 'Home Rule for Ireland', resistance to the movement for 'Disestablishment and Disendowment of the Anglican Church in Wales', and 'Abolition of the House of Lords'. As described earlier, in an effort to win over the populace, the dames went around knocking on doors, and various social and entertainment events were organised, often held in the grounds of the local gentry.

Needless to say, the primarily Nonconformist Liberals were less than impressed, and local newspapers continued to carry many mocking articles, as elucidated by the Rt Hon. Osborne Morgan: 'You have to fight against jobbery, snobbery and the weird sisters of the Primrose League.' In 1887, Sir Henry James' speech to a Liberal Unionist Conference in Manchester provoked a response published in the *Wrexham Advertiser* on 12 February, 1887. This included a number of scathing remarks:

> Not all the united wisdom of all the legislators we possess, will ever be able to produce a law which will be effective to prevent women from influencing the votes of electors, unless, indeed, all the women in the land are to be locked up in harems on the Turkish system …
>
> If he admits that women are manifesting a great capacity for influencing the minds of electors, is not that tantamount to saying that they do not understand a great deal about politics? Or does he really believe that the male creature is so weak in his political convictions, or so careless about the effect of his vote, that his adherence to one party or the other may be purchased with a smile?

Despite objections from some Tory party members the league officially ceased in 2004, although a couple of isolated pockets still remain. The league was very active during the Disraeli/Gladstone premierships, and their dislike of one another is highlighted by one of Disraeli's scathing comments about Gladstone. Written on a blind at Disraeli's old home, Hughenden Manor, will be found the following quotation: 'If Gladstone were to fall in the Thames and drown that would be a tragedy. If someone rescued him that would be a disaster.' It is not certain whether the 'grand old man' would have been particularly amused to find that his burial spot in Westminster Abbey is next to a statue of Disraeli, particularly as, on the anniversary of Disraeli's death, members of the Primrose League laid primroses at the foot of the statue.

The second Conservative-supporting organisation came into being as a result of a speech by Aneurin Bevan on 4 July 1948. Speaking to a Labour rally in Manchester, and referring to the nation's poor state of health, he stated: 'That is why no cajolery can eradicate from my heart a deep, burning hatred for the Tory party that inflicted those experiences on me. So far as I am concerned they are lower than vermin. They condemned millions of first class people to semi-starvation …'

The reaction to this speech provoked an outcry across the country. One newspaper carried the headline: 'The Man who Hates 8,093,858 People', reflecting the fact that this was the number of votes cast for the Conservative party in the 1945 election. Bevan's house, in Clifton Place, London, had the words 'Vermin Place – Home of a Loud Mouth' daubed across the front.

Other direct action was required, and the younger members of the Conservative party took up the baton and formed an organisation called the 'Vermin Club'. The two principle aims were defined as (1) To organise the anti-socialist electorate, and (2) To publicise the danger of socialism. The Fourth of July was to be celebrated as 'Vermin Day'. They took the rat as their emblem

Vermin Club badge. (Jonathan Evans, MP)

and their badges carried a picture of the rat and the word 'vermin'. A hierarchy was established and recruitment of members was reflected in which badges you were entitled to wear; for recruiting ten members your badge would carry the words 'vile vermin' and for twenty-five new members, you would be allowed to wear a badge with 'very vile vermin' engraved on it. Local branches were called 'nests' and these comprised 200 members. Life membership cost 2*s* with the fees donated to Cancer Research, and the club's 1949 Christmas cards carried the words 'An Anti-Socialist Vermin Helping Cancer Research'.

At its peak it had over 120,000 members, and the author was told that there was a branch in Mold and, whilst a local garage owner wore the basic badge, this was hidden under his coat lapel! One former Chief Rat was the late Baroness Thatcher. The club archives are held at the Bodleian Library, Oxford, and provide a wonderful insight into post-war politics in Britain.

QUAKERS: THOMAS WYNNE AND THE FOUNDING OF PHILADELPHIA AND PENNSYLVANIA

What is apparent from any research into Flintshire is the influence of religious Nonconformity throughout the county, and earlier stories have covered different aspects of the various religious movements. The parish of Ysceifiog appears in the Domesday Book of 1086, where it is spelled as 'Schiuiau', and it is believed that a church existed there in the fifth century.

As was the accepted practice, people worshipped in the parish church, and Thomas Wynne of Bron Fadog, born on 27 July 1627, was no different. Baptised as a member of the established church, he was brought up as a Protestant,

The current Ysceifiog church. (Mary Bamborough)

but in the religious turmoil of the English Civil Wars of the 1640s, he felt spiritually abandoned and was less than impressed with the messages coming from the pulpits. In the mid-1650s, he became acquainted with John ap John, described as a Quaker apostle, and in 1655 he married a Quaker, Martha Buttall – two events that transformed his life as he embraced Quakerism.

From an early age Wynne had a great interest in the work of local surgeons, and often played truant from school to watch surgeons practicing their art. At the age of 10, his father died and as his mother could not afford to pay for medical training, Wynne was apprenticed to a cooper. Despite this initial setback, he pursued his medical studies during his spare time and, with the guidance of a Quaker surgeon, he qualified as a barber surgeon in the late 1650s. Sometime in the mid-1660s he established a practice in nearby Caerwys.

During the period of the Restoration of the monarchy, members of the Anglican Church sought retribution against Nonconformists, and Quakers were a prime target. The enactment of the Quaker Act of 1662 was designed to eradicate what was seen as a heretical sect, and Wynne and others spent a number of years in Ruthin Gaol as a result of their beliefs.

However, this did not stop the founder of Quakerism, George Fox, from recruiting new members throughout Flintshire, and Bron Fadog became one of two centres for Quakers. Wynne, after his release from gaol, continued with his mission and in 1677 published *The Antiquity of the Quakers*, which brought scathing responses from his opponents.

King Charles II, on 4 March 1681, issued a charter to the Quaker William Penn for a province in the New World that we now know as Pennsylvania. Amongst the Flintshire Quakers wishing to take advantage of the land on offer was Thomas Wynne, and he purchased 5,000 acres for an initial sum of £100. In view of the ongoing hostility towards the Quakers, Wynne made the decision to emigrate and he and Penn sailed to America on board the *Welcome*, which was carrying approximately 2,000 people as part of a fleet of twenty-three ships.

During the journey smallpox broke out, and Wynne's medical skills were required, but sadly at least thirty passengers had died by the time the ship arrived in New Castle, Delaware, on 27 October 1682. The Wynnes settled in Philadelphia and initially a street was named in his honour, but this ultimately became Chestnut Street, and remains so to this day.

Wynne made one visit back to the United Kingdom, including his home county of Flintshire, but whilst in London attending a funeral, he and fellow Quakers were arrested and charged with riotous assembly with force and arms. The magistrates found these peace-loving and pacifist Quakers guilty of the unwarranted charges, and Wynne and the others were fined and spent three months in Newgate Prison. After his release in April 1685, he returned to

Caerwys and found himself before the Great Sessions for failing to attend church for the previous three months in August of that year.

In August 1686 he returned to Pennsylvania, with the hope that he could follow the teachings of his church unhindered and without persecution. Thomas Wynne became one of the pillars of the Society of Friends in the USA, and served in many public offices. He was appointed Speaker of the newly formed Provincial Assembly, represented his county in the assembly, and also served as a provincial judge for the two years prior to his death in 1692. He is buried in Friends Burial Ground at Duckett's Farm, Philadelphia, and without doubt he can be considered one of the founding fathers of Pennsylvania.

Hazel Formby, in her publication *A History of Ysceifiog*, tells of another legacy: 'the street plan of Philadelphia is said to have been based on that of Caerwys'.

QUARTER SESSIONS AND THE ROLLS-ROYCE

The Courts of Quarter Sessions of England and Wales were local courts first established in 1388, and took their name from the four annual sittings of the court. Along with the Assizes, they were abolished in 1972 and replaced by Crown Courts. The courts were held in Flint until the late 1770s, before being transferred to Mold. From 1834, until replaced by the new Law Courts in 1967, the sessions were held in the court house on Chester Street. The court house was the location of the trial associated with the Mold Riots, and it is said that bullet holes from a volley fired by soldiers during that dark day can still be seen in the stonework.

However, it is in the 1960s that a most unusual occurrence took place and caused much amusement to members of the legal profession and passers-by. In what is now Mold Bus Station stood the county council offices and, as parking was always at a premium, particularly during court sittings, this was strictly controlled by Ivor Jones and Alan Whitley. On the day in question Justin Price, a Chester and North Wales barrister, had parked his vintage Rolls-Royce (or Bentley) while he attended the court, and it is believed he had 'crossed swords' with the two guardians of the car park.

The circumstances surrounding what happened next vary from one eyewitness to another, but all are agreed on the conclusion. It appears that Mr Price attempted to exit the area by driving down the steps from the court house onto Chester Street. Much to the great amusement of all the onlookers, the vintage car became wedged on the steps and all attempts to move it up or down were doomed to failure. The car spent the night on the steps until Trevor Harley, from the nearby garage, arranged for it to be lifted free, much to the relief of the red-faced lawyer.

RACING – HOLYWELL RACECOURSE, A PICKPOCKET AND A CASTLE

Amongst the favourite pastimes of the local gentry were horseracing and hunting and, prior to its popularity being overtaken by Chester racecourse, race meetings held at the course at Holywell were high on the social calendar of many families. The racecourse, located on Holywell common, was over 2 miles in length and operated from 1767 through to the mid-nineteenth century.

An edition of *The Times* in 1796 advises that, at the next Chester Races:

> Gentlemen of the Holywell Hunt Society & Racecourse, have advertised a sweepstake of Five Guineas to be run for Cart Horses in a broad wheel [6in width] cart, over the last mile of the course. The carts are to be of a similar weight and structure and are to carry 4cwt each, exclusive of Charioteers.

The charioteers were to wear smock frocks of different colours.

At Holywell, racegoers wanting an easy life are believed to have built a house nearby, enabling gambling and drinking downstairs and, local legend suggests, 'ladies' entertaining upstairs. True or an urban myth?

In 1831, a horse named 'Pickpocket' (born in 1828, and owned by Sir Richard Buckley) won a race at Holywell, and then followed this up in 1833 by winning the Chester Cup. As a result, the original name of his house was changed to Pickpocket Hall. Confirmation of the link can be found in the following advert in the *North Wales Chronicle* of 23 May 1886:

> Lot 3 of an Auction
>
> A genteel COTTAGE RESIDENCE, called Pickpocket Hall, with out-offices, gardens, pleasure grounds, and lands, immediately surrounding the same, situate adjoining the old Holywell race course, fronting the road from Holywell to Avon Wen, containing in the whole 28 perches or thereabouts, and occupied by Captain Sandoe.
>
> Lot 3 was leased to Sir Richard Buckley, Bart. MP for fifty years, seventeen years of which are unexpired on 30 November, at a low yearly reserved rent of £10.

Pickpocket Hall. (David Rowe)

Racing also played a major role in the building of Halkyn Castle. The house, designed by John Buckler, was built 1824–1828 and further extended in 1886. The 2nd Earl Grosvenor and his guests, attending Holywell Races, were in the habit of staying at the Golden Lion & White Horse in Holywell (now the HSBC bank), but on one occasion they discovered a commercial traveller staying there who refused to vacate the hotel. As a result, it is claimed that this provoked Earl Grosvenor, by now 1st Marquess of Westminster, to commission the building of the castle.

RAILWAYS, RABBITS AND COMFORT BREAKS

Clergymen of all denominations are accustomed to people recounting experiences in their lives but a retired Methodist minister, Reverend Alan Cliff, was more than surprised at a story told to him by the last surviving employee of the Great Central Railway. The railway was purchased by the Wrexham, Mold & Connah's Quay Railway in 1905, before it became part of LNER in 1923.

There was always a competitive edge between passenger and goods crews, and both sets would happily put one over on the other. Whilst passenger trains had to run to predetermined timetables, goods trains had no such requirement. Much to the disgust, or jealousy, of their passenger train colleagues, the goods train staff would, on their outward journey, set snares for rabbits and then on the return collect them. Wages were then enhanced by selling their catch in and around Wrexham Central Station.

However, not to be outdone, the crews on passenger trains plying the Wrexham, Mold & Connah's Quay route to Bidston/Seacombe found a method of supplementing their wages. As the trains were non-corridor trains, 'comfort' stops at stations were required, and the guards would charge first-class passengers 6*d* and second-class passengers 3*d* to ensure the train would be held until they returned, much relieved.

ROMANS IN CAERGWRLE AND HOPE?

We have indisputable evidence that the Romans were active throughout Flintshire, evidenced by a farm settlement at Flint and the remains of their lead mining activities. This mining activity is best highlighted by the discovery of a bar of lead in Carmel in 1950, when the new school was being built. More commonly known as the 'Carmel Pig', the original can be found at the National Museum of Wales, whilst replicas are in Carmel School and the Grosvenor Museum, Chester.

In 2006, an episode of Channel 4's *Time Team* series entitled 'Early Bath' carried out a dig at Frith. Whilst the number of finds was quite small, they did turn up a brooch and bone dice. The episode featured Tony Robinson proudly displaying the dice in the local pub, and the dice is now in the possession of the Flintshire Museums Service.

In 2013, builders at the Croes Atti site at Oakenholt uncovered a Roman lead foundry. This comprised of buildings, together with many industrial features, including hearths and other processing areas associated with the Roman exploitation of local lead ores which are found on Halkyn Mountain. The many finds included pottery fragments, lead, coins and glass, and these were discovered during a three-week dig by archaeologists.

However, we do have a mystery at Caergwrle and Hope. Did the Romans have a travelling camp, similar to the illustration, in the area of Llwyn-Owen Farm in Fagl Lane? In the *Annals and Antiques of the Counties and County Families of Wales* it is stated that 'there is reason to believe that it was a place of note in Roman times' and quotes as its source the Elizabethan antiquarian, historian and topographer, William Camden. During research carried out for a topographical and historical survey of Great Britain and Ireland called *Britannia*, Camden noted that he

A Roman marching camp. (Graham Sumner – © Roman Fort Project)

discovered a hypocaust, 6 yards by 5 yards, hewn out of solid rock, and that on some of the tiles were inscribed the letters LEGIO XX. As the 20th Legion was stationed at Chester for some time, did Caergwrle serve as an outpost?

For centuries the area has been populated – a Bronze Age shale bowl dating from 2000 BC was found on the banks of the River Dee; flint tools dating from 250,000–8,000 BC have been discovered locally; Caer Estyn hill fort was built during the Iron Age; a Roman coin was found locally; part of Wat's Dyke runs through the area and, in 1277, Dafydd ap Gruffydd started the building of Caergwrle Castle. These links and strong military position would certainly appeal to the Romans, but as yet, their presence has not been conclusively proven to the satisfaction of all. With the aim of proving the link, the exciting 'Roman Fort Project' is, at the time of writing, in its early stages. Amongst its aims are plans to reconstruct a first-century Roman marching camp and Iron Age settlement, which can be used for research, educational and recreational purposes.

ROYAL FLYING CORPS – 'MOTH' EYTON

The early military aviator saw himself as a form of medieval knight, and certainly during the First World War the old rules of chivalry applied between the pilots of the opposing flying corps.

The Royal Flying Corps was formed in May 1912 but, due to the superiority of German aircraft, over 800 British planes were lost and 252 crew killed in the period July–November 1916. Despite having a short life expectancy, the corps was never short of volunteers, and Charles Stanford 'Sandy' Wynne-Eyton of the Leeswood and Tower estates, was no exception. Returning home from Siam (Thailand) where he had been employed, he was commissioned into the Royal Field Artillery. Wounded and gassed in France, he transferred to the Royal Flying Corps in 1915, eventually attaining the rank of major. In the 1918 New Year's Honours list he was awarded the DSO.

On the formation of the Royal Air Force, he transferred and remained in the RAF until 1926 when, with the rank of squadron leader, he resigned his commission and went to live in Rhodesia (now Zimbabwe). As well as tobacco farming, he was the first flying instructor in Salisbury, Rhodesia, and the first private owner of an aircraft – a Cirrus Moth. It is from this wonderful aeroplane that he acquired his nickname of 'Moth' Eyton' (pronounced 'eaten').

'Moth' Eyton's wedding. (Charles Wynne-Eyton)

When the Rhodesia-based Wilson Airways commenced in mid-1929, he began working for the newly established airline. On 26 May 1930, he registered a De Havilland DH80 Puss Moth, registration G-AAXI, which had been built as a special long-range single-seater for a proposed solo transatlantic crossing. On taking off from Lester Field, St John's, Newfoundland, on 6 July 1930, the plane crashed, leaving Wynne-Eyton badly injured and his plane completely destroyed by fire. He recovered from his injuries and, on the outbreak of the Second World War, he re-enlisted in the RAF, with the rank of wing commander, and continued to fly on active service.

Subsequently awarded an Air Force Cross, his luck finally ran out when he and seven others were killed when their Liberator II, of 144 MU (Middle East Command), crashed into a mountain near Autun in France, en route to RAF Lyneham from the Middle East on 14 November 1944. He is buried in the Choloy War Cemetery, in north-eastern France.

Charles was not the only one of the family to serve in the RFC. His elder brother, Robert Mainwaring Wynne-Eyton, was farming in British Columbia when war was declared in 1914. He immediately enlisted in the British Columbia Force and served in the Duke of Westminster's Armoured Cars in the Egyptian and Senussi campaigns. He transferred to the Royal Flying Corps, and served in Serbia, where he was wounded, and later in Belgium, where he was shot down. Ditching into the sea, it is said that he saved his observer's life before they were picked up by a Dutch ship and interned in Holland for the last two months of the war. Mentioned in dispatches three times, he was also awarded the Military Cross.

The aviation link continues with the family, as a step-brother, Arthur George Neville Wynne-Eyton, was a wartime production test pilot for Short Bros & Harland Ltd and tested the last Stirling bomber to come off the production line at Aldergrove. After the war he became resident instructor and secretary to the Ulster Flying Club, but sadly he was killed in a car accident in Co. Down on 12 July 1954. He was held in such esteem that the club cancelled its first 'At Home' scheduled for 31 July 1954.

S

SACRILEGIOUS ACTS AND ST MARY THE VIRGIN PARISH CHURCH, MOLD

Throughout the centuries the parish church of Mold has undergone many changes. The building of the current church began in the late fifteenth century, under its patron Lady Margaret Beaufort, Countess of Richmond and Derby, and mother of Henry VII.

The various modifications and alterations to the church, along with changes to the status of the established church within Wales, have not always met with universal approval. Whilst no doubt letters were sent to newspapers and representations were made to the authorities, it is unlikely that such protests were reflected in the fabric of the building, as they were during the restoration of the south porch in 1911, by Prothero, Phillpot & Barnard, a firm of architects from Cheltenham.

Grotesque Lloyd George. (Pam Ratcliffe)

Some of the building work at this time was financed by the Davies-Cooke family of Gwysaney, and the family considered that two people, one living and one dead, were responsible for gross sacrilegious acts against the church. One was Oliver Cromwell, whose troopers during the Civil War are reported as having stabled their horses inside the church.

The second was the former prime minister and fervent Nonconformist, David Lloyd George, who actively campaigned for the disestablishment and disendowment of the Anglican Church in Wales. This particular campaign was spearheaded by a Denbigh Methodist deacon and publisher, Thomas Gee. He and his many supporters disagreed with the fact that Anglicans in Wales enjoyed legal privileges over the Nonconformist majority. The payment of tithes, entitling the Anglican Church to a tenth of people's income, irrespective of whether they actually attended church, was a particular bone of contention. This ultimately led to confrontation and violence between the authorities and the chapel-going majority, and was known as the 'Tithe Wars'. Many of the predominately Anglican gentry saw this as a challenge to their authority and objected vehemently to the proposal for disestablishment, which ultimately came to pass in 1920.

So what better way for Davies-Cooke to repay these two characters than by incorporating grotesques/chimera into the building in their likeness? Chimera is derived from an Italian word *babuino*, meaning baboon, and the *Illustrated Dictionary of British Churches* defines grotesques as 'depicting human figures or faces, demons, animals or other mythical creatures, often with exaggerated fierce or humorous expressions. Some are obviously meant to lampoon'. So where will these grotesques be found? Facing the south porch, look up at the left hand pinnacle and there you will see the heads of Cromwell and Lloyd George with what appears to be a serpent coming out from their necks.

SHIPBUILDING AND SHIPPING – FROM CONNAH'S QUAY TO TREASURE ISLAND

It is believed that when Charles Kingsley visited Flintshire, he wrote a poem entitled 'The Sands of Dee':

> Oh Mary, go and call the cattle home,
> And call the cattle home,
> And call the cattle home,
> Across the sands of Dee;
> The western wind was wild and dank with foam,
> And all along went she.

This tells the story of a girl called Mary who, whilst calling the cattle home, is drowned. The Dee is notorious for its quicksand and currents, so over the centuries there have been many deaths of unwary and unlucky people.

However, the river has also provided a living for many families, legal or otherwise, and the 1861 census for the township of Wepre shows that out of a total of 708 residents, a high percentage owed their livelihood to marine activities and, on the day of the census, seventy-one males and three females were temporarily absent 'at sea'. Further back, in 1795, Thomas Pennant reports on the volume of wheat and rye being shipped out of Wepre and Bagillt. At that time Wepre was responsible for 65 per cent of the shipment of rye coming out of various ports, including Chester, along the North Wales coastline.

Shipping and associated shipbuilding was a major industry, particularly in Connah's Quay, which was also the home of many sea captains and ship owners, whose descendants still live in Flintshire. One notable ship, built in 1900 at the Ferguson & Baird yard in Connah's Quay for leading local ship owners the Coppack family, was the pictured *Kathleen & May*. The vessel was originally called after Captain John Coppack's two daughters, Lizzie and May. Subsequently she was sold on to Martin Fleming of Youghall, Co. Cork, who renamed it after *his* two daughters, Kathleen and May.

The *Onedin* vessel. (Paul Davies)

When she was bought by Captain Jewell of Appledore, Devon, in 1931, he retained her name and she was fitted with an engine. She continued to trade until 1961, when she was left to rot. In 1968, she was 'discovered' by the Duke of Edinburgh. The duke subsequently created the Maritime Trust, and this body purchased the vessel and restored her, such that she appeared as the *Charlotte Rose* in the TV series *The Onedin Line*. The series had ninety-one episodes and was screened between 1971 and 1980.

Later she was privately purchased by Steve Clarke, who carried out further restoration works. In 2008, *The Times* reported that, 'with our desire to follow a green agenda the *Kathleen & May* has returned to her original purpose as a cargo vessel carrying 30,000 bottles of wine for Languedoc-Roussillon winegrowers to Dublin'. The refurbished vessel was at the head of the 'Avenue of Sail' in the Thames Pageant celebrating the Queen's Diamond Jubilee in 2012, and was moored opposite the royal barge. The vessel, now based in Liverpool, is open to the public.

Another ship used in the movies and associated with Connah's Quay, but actually built by Nicholson & Marsh of Lancaster in 1887, was the three-masted schooner *Ryelands*. Initially designed for the coastal trade, she later had an engine installed, but her claim to fame is twofold. In 1949 she was seen as the *Hispaniola* in Walt Disney's *Treasure Island*, and in the 1954 movie *Moby Dick* she featured as the Nantucket whaler *Pequod*, skippered by Captain Ahab. (The ship's name is believed to have originated from the Native American tribe called the 'Pequot'.)

The last years of her life were spent as a tourist attraction at Scarborough and Morecambe where, in 1972, she was totally destroyed by fire.

SCULPTORS, PAST AND PRESENT – ABSTRACT, RELIGIOUS AND SECULAR

When most of us think of sculptures, we either think of the great Renaissance works of art, politicians or the local benefactor whose statue can be found in some prominent place in our towns and parks. We also glance at the various memorials in churches without appreciating the standing of the person who created the works of art.

The current church of St Michael & All Angels, Nannerch, is the third on the site and contains a large and impressive monument to Charlotte Theophile Mostyn (*née* Digby) who had married Richard Henry Mostyn of Penbedw. Charlotte was the great-granddaughter of Sir Everard Digby, a Gunpowder Plot conspirator who, in 1605, had visited St Winefride's Well, Holywell. Although Sir Everard was executed for his part in the plot, his son redeemed the family reputation and estates, and we come full circle with the Flintshire link when Charlotte married a Mostyn and her sister Margaretta married Sir John Conway of Bodrhyddan. Charlotte died in 1694 and the renowned sculptor Grinling Gibbons was commissioned to produce the monument we see at rear of the church.

Grinling Gibbons (1648–1721) was born and worked as an apprentice in Amsterdam before moving to England in the 1660s. Widely regarded as the finest wood carver working in Britain, whilst most of his work was in wood, he did also produce works in stone. A favourite of King Charles II, he became known as the 'King's carver', and his work can also be found in St Paul's Cathedral, Hampton Court Palace, Petworth House and Westminster Abbey.

Grinling Gibbons' work. (David Rowe)

The link with the Digby family did not die out. After the purchase of the estate by the Buddicom family, the last member of the family to live at the now demolished Penbedw Hall was Venetia Digby Buddicom. The name Venetia came from her grandmother Venetia Stanley, who came from a branch of the former lords of Mold and Hawarden, the Stanleys' Earl of Derby line.

In an earlier story, mention was made of the sculptor William Theed the Younger's work at Gwernaffield church. However, the religious tradition of sculpting is not a thing of the past. Locally it continues today with Fr Rory Geoghegan, a Jesuit priest at St Beuno's, Tremeirchion, who is responsible for many fine religious works in and beyond the county boundaries.

He initially trained in fine art and after an illness about twelve to fourteen years ago he was given the opportunity to use his training. He initially produces a small model of the subject in clay or plaster prior to producing the full-size sculpture. In 2013, his plaster sculpture of the 'Reservation of Eucharist' depicting the seated figure of Christ was installed in St David's Catholic church, Mold. The quality of his work is fully recognised in a book entitled *Biblical Art from Wales* by Martin O'Kane and John Morgan Guy. In the introduction, Fr Geoghegan makes the following comments:

> My sculptures, which might be described as contemporary sacred art, have been seen in various churches in England and Wales. There has been encouraging interest in the subjects I have made my own. My intention has been to appeal to people who spend times of prayerful consideration at St Beuno's, where they are seen around the house. So I encourage people 'to spend time being with them', explore all sides of the piece. Wander around them. Make your time with any one piece a time of discovery and personal enquiry.

Abstract sculpture leaves many people scratching their heads and wondering about the meaning of such pieces. Our next sculptor and writer was gifted in many media and styles, but his Flintshire legacy can be found outside the court rooms in Mold Law Courts in the form of two abstract sculptures with a religious link – 'Justice' and 'Mercy'.

Made from Welsh slate and Sicilian marble they are defined as follows: 'Justice' is an exercise in balance, symmetry and measure. The scale of measure at the top can also be interpreted as a crown. Other images implied in the design are the shield and the sword. The image is seen as impartial, imperturbable and unbending. The horizontals are twelve in number – the jury. In 'Mercy', the twelve have adopted a quite different aspect. Here the twelve, in a kind of winged or petalled concentric design, bend or stoop towards a formalised image of the human family and the thorns and punishment fall away before the intercession. The tears of Christ are shed upon the image. These were produced by the Tyneside-born sculptor Jonah Jones who, incidentally, attended the same Jarrow School as the author, although in the latter's case it was a considerable number of years afterwards.

Although Jonah was a conscientious objector for much of the Second World War, he nevertheless volunteered to serve first in the Non-Combatant Corps and then as a medic in 224 Parachute Field Ambulance of the 6th Airborne Division. Jonah described this unit as 'filled up with an odd assortment of awkward squads; rationalists, vegans, Quakers, Methodists, Jehovah's Witnesses, anarchists and rebels of no known grouping, among them artists, writers and designers – all "nutters" in the regimental sergeant-major's view'. During his military service he was one of the first medics to enter Bergen-Belsen concentration camp, scenes of which remained with him for the rest of his life.

As well as carrying out his own works, he taught and was an external examiner at many colleges of art: he was director of Ireland's National College of Art and Design and a faculty member with the British School at Rome. A close friend of Sir Clough Williams-Ellis and Sir Kyffin Williams, Jonah established a workshop at Tremadog, and amongst his pieces at Portmeirion is a bust of Williams-Ellis. A catalogue of his main works written by his son, Peter, can be found in the book *Jonah Jones – An Artist's Life*. A remarkable man, who became a national figure in Wales and who fully deserves his entry in *The Welsh Academy Encyclopedia of Wales*.

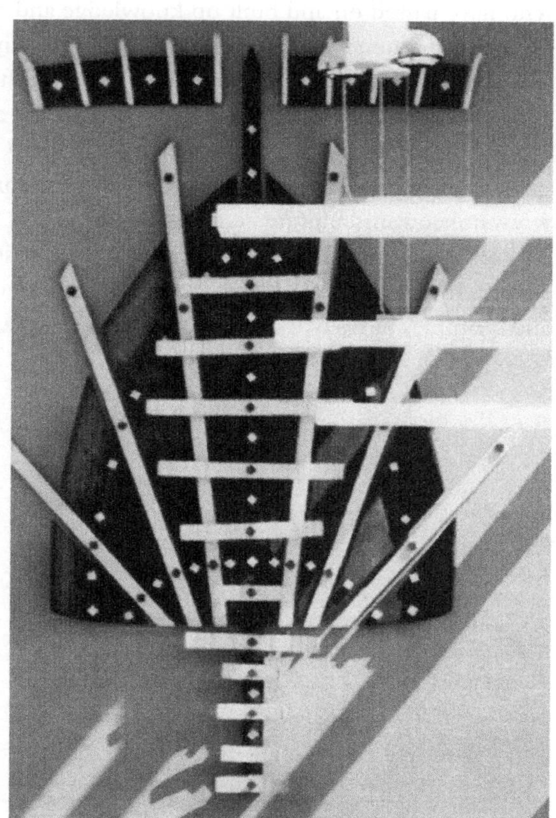

The Law Courts' abstract sculpture. (David Rowe)

Resting quarrymen. (Tom Wood)

The next sculptor is very much alive and active, and passing through Brynford crossroads the observer's attention is drawn to a wooden sculpture of three resting figures by local artist Michael Owens, of Caerwys. The sculpture represents the history of extensive quarrying in Flintshire, and the figures represent workers who have passed on and built up knowledge and expertise over each generation. Quarrymen often worked alone with large noisy machines, and the working day was divided by breaks rather than the divides on the clock face. Such breaks were very important and allowed the men to eat, relax and socialise. However, for the current visitor, the sculpture also acts as a sundial. Owens' work can also be found on the All Wales coastal path at Bettisfield, and for full details of his work go to www.mikeowenssculpture.co.uk.

Works on the Flintshire section of the coastal path, Holywell and Flint, are attributable to the Nottinghamshire-based sculptor Michael Johnson, and examples of his work can be viewed on www.michaeljohnsonsculptor.co.uk.

T

TEMPERANCE AND FORESTERS' HALL COCOA ROOMS, BAGILLT

In these days of 'expensive' but clean water we tend to forget that, in the nineteenth century, the quality of water was not all it should be and therefore the drinking of beer avoided badly infected and even life-threatening water supplies.

The majority of men were also involved in manual work, and it is understandable that miners or quarrymen coming off Halkyn, or Nercwys Mountain in winter would head for somewhere with a big blazing fire and good *craic.* In some cases, men would be paid in public houses and as a result the greater part of limited family budgets would end up being spent on alcohol.

In the early nineteenth century, the effects of the 'evil drink' were recognised, and temperance societies began to spring up throughout the country. The aims of this movement were particularly adopted by quite a few branches of Nonconformity. In the 1847 report on 'The State of Education in Wales', drinking came in for particular comment: 'The prevailing vice of the part of Flintshire being drunkenness.' Whilst this particular comment was aimed at Bagillt, similar remarks, in this report and others, were made about other towns or villages throughout the county.

Some residents of Bagillt recognised that something needed to be done to change this situation and, whilst plans for a workingman's club were produced, it was not until December 1877 that the project moved on. The decision was made to combine the club with an alternative to public houses – a 'cocoa house'. Under the will of Mr Ellis Eyton, £200 was left for this purpose, the Duke of Westminster gave £25, and around 200 workmen bought shares at £1 each. These funds, along with other donations, allowed the construction of the building under the supervision of the architect Mr Bibby, of Flint, to commence in May 1878.

The *Cheshire Observer* of 13 September 1879, reported on the official opening of the Bagillt Workingmen's Club and Cocoa House, describing it thus: 'The refreshment department is on the ground floor, above which are club-rooms and a large assembly room. Billiard and reading rooms are also included.' This was the first establishment of its kind in Wales.

Members of the Oddfellows, Druids and the Bagillt Foresters' Club No 841, who had raised a mortgage of £800 towards the cost of the building, marched through the town accompanied by various bands to the railway station, where they met invited guests. The societies escorted the guests back to the building and they were given a guided tour and a luncheon. The official opening ceremony was performed in front of the building, with speeches being made from the upper window. A letter was read out from Lord Richard Grosvenor MP, who had been unable to attend. In his letter he stated:

> From experience of houses already opened, I do believe that at last the right thing has been hit upon to check in some measure the curse of drunkenness; and I have no doubt it will not only promote good amongst the customers, but will be a good investment for the shareholders, of whom I am one.

Foresters' Hall, Bagillt. (David Rowe)

Amongst the guests was Mr J. Roberts, MP for Flint Boroughs, who was responsible for the Sunday Closing Act being enforced. Following the opening of the house it initially prospered and, in December 1880, there was even a suggestion of forming a Parliamentary Debating Club for Holywell, Flint and Bagillt.

Sadly, the Cocoa House was short-lived and, far from investors getting a good return on their investments, the company went into liquidation in 1885. The decision was made to convert the building into a shop and assembly room, better known as Foresters' Hall, and once again money was raised to allow the £200 costs to be covered. The shop was purchased by a pawnbroker, whilst the billiard room and assembly rooms remained in constant use. The shop was eventually converted to the village sub-post office, before it closed in the 1990s. After standing empty for some time, the building was finally converted to residential units, so at least this wonderful building has been preserved. Next time you are travelling up Bagillt High Street, look out for a three-storied building that has many tales to tell.

This was not the end of temperance organisations, and in Hawarden we find the People's House Refreshment Association taking over the Glynne Arms. They were licensees from 1906 to the mid-1950s, and although alcohol was available, this was not displayed and customers would have to ask for liquor, which was sold at inflated prices. Even the *New York Times* on 5 September 1904 ran an article on the movement, suggesting that the US followed suit.

So, who was behind such an organisation? The Bishop of Chester supported its aims, as did a Quaker philanthropist, called Charles Booth (1840–1916). Born in Liverpool, Booth formed his own shipping line in 1866, in partnership with his brother Alfred. The ships were named after saints, and the company became part of Blue Star Shipping in 1975. The line operated a service between the UK and northern Brazil and the Amazon. Booth was also extremely concerned about the working man, and subsequently produced a number of reports, including one in 1889, where he identified that 35 per cent of the families residing in London were living in a state of abject poverty. He also led a movement for the establishment of old age pensions for everyone.

Another organisation very active throughout Flintshire well into the 1900s was the Band of Hope, a temperance organisation for working-class children, which was founded in Leeds in 1847. All members took a pledge of total abstinence and were taught the 'evils of drink'. Members were enrolled from the age of 6 and met once a week to listen to lectures and participate in activities. Further encouragement was given in the form of treats and outings. However, despite the perceived benefits of 'signing the pledge', a newspaper article in 1838 reported that this had not gone down well with proprietors of a colliery. They issued a notice stating 'as a duty which they owe to the Agricultural Interest of the country as well as the welfare of the public in general, they had come to the resolution not to employ any Teetotallers'. Those not retracting the pledge were sacked!

TOMPION-MOSTYN CLOCK, RAILWAY TIME AND THE GRAND NATIONAL

In a 2013 conversation with Lord Mostyn, he passed a remark that he had just been to London to wind 'the clock'. This reference to the clock meant nothing to the author, so further research was necessary.

Lord Mostyn was referring to the Tompion-Mostyn clock, which is 73.6cm high x 34cm wide x 24.5cm deep, and was made for King William III by probably Britain's greatest watch and clockmaker, Thomas Tompion (1639–1713). He became Master of the Worshipful Company of Clockmakers in 1703 and, due to the royal patronage of both Charles II and William III, he was the first clockmaker to be buried in Westminster Abbey. Regarded by many as the father of English clock making, his importance is also recognised by the fact that the Worshipful Company still maintains the family cottage in Ickwell, Bedfordshire.

The Tompion-Mostyn clock was produced in the late 1690s. Made from ebony and richly decorated with silver, it is a magnificent example of the clockmaker's art. This particular clock was a favourite of King William, and on his death it was willed to a Gentleman of the Bedchamber, the Earl of Romney. It eventually came into the hands of the Mostyn family and was moved to Mostyn Hall in 1825. A note written on 3 May 1903 states: 'The clock was specially made for King William III by Tompion; at a cost, it is said, of £1500. It was kept in a room in Kensington Palace which the King occupied as a Bedchamber …'

The Tompion-Mostyn Clock.
(The Trustees of the British Museum)

A special feature of the clock is that it runs for twelve months on a single winding, and it is this fact that led to a tradition, begun in 1793, of keeping records of the annual winding ceremony. In 1982, the clock was put on the market with a valuation of around £1 million. As it was considered a national treasure and therefore likely to be subject to export regulations, it was saved for the nation for an undisclosed figure. Acquired by the British Museum, they have maintained the tradition of an annual winding ceremony, and this is what Lord Mostyn was referring to during our conversation.

The winding records have, throughout the centuries, been maintained in a 'Winding Book' and the British Museum has kindly provided me with a transcript prepared by a former curator, Jeremy Evans. The book lists all the people who have wound the clock, and also provides additional supplementary information, extracts of which follow.

Setting the Time

Prior to standard time being set Tompion, like many of the great clockmakers, also made sundials to 'collect' the time so that they could set the time on their timepieces. Only six of his sundials are known to exist, three in private hands and the others being at Kew Palace, Hampton Court Palace and Bath's Pump Room. As you are no doubt aware, this method of collection meant a considerable variance in times across the country, and with the coming of the railways this played havoc with timetables for long-distance travel. In the 1840s, the decision was made to standardise time to that of London, and it was set at Greenwich by the Royal Observatory. However, it is not until 22 October 1859 that the winding book has a reference to setting the Tompion-Mostyn clock to 'railway time'.

Cold Weather

The clock appears to have been susceptible to cold weather and without sufficient warmth it would simply stop:

1823 – The clock was wound up on ye 15th of Feby1823 by Mr Pitt of Duke St who had cleaned it – it had gone regularly for 10 year but had stopped ye last Month in ye very hard Weather in Jany 1823.

1838 – It had stopped before Xmas but during the hard frost we did not wind it – as extreme cold frequently stops it.

1860 – During the severe cold in March 1860 – the Clock stopped again.

In 1961, the entry advises how this problem has been overcome: 'The electric fire keeps the Drawing room well aired, and warm, which I contend has a great effect on this wonderful clock.' Two years later, the entry records that the problem had finally been solved. 'The heat in the drawing room has been well maintained, as I have two permanent heaters and as well as the electric fire if wanted and the whole house has been oil fired for central heating this winter.'

Annual Winding Parties

The winding of the clock has been recorded since 1793, but initially details were written on individual sheets of paper – the entries in the winding book commenced in 1891. There is a gap between 1908 and 1931, and the reason is given in the following 1908 entry: '"King William' was wound up on the evening of Augt. 20th having run for 12 months as the clock had to be wound up early as all the family were to leave Liverpool the next day for Canada by the *Empress of Britain*.'

The first entry in 1931 makes reference to the family practice of having a party to coincide with the running of the Grand National: 'This was the evening of the break up of our Grand National Party "Grakle" having won the Grand National (on the Friday) …' The practice of recording the winners continued, and the 1938 entry suggests a little smugness on the part of Lord Mostyn: 'King William Clock was wound up this evening of the Grand National on March 25th. I was the only member of our party who backed the winner "Battleship" at 40 to 1; an American-bred horse of 15h …'

Guest Winders

From 1874, detailed information on the winders was recorded, with the first entry being on 10 October 1874: 'This clock was wound on Oct. 10 1874 by Harriet Roberts, House Keeper at Mostyn, in the presence of Lady Mostyn Honbles Harriot, Essex and Katherine Mostyn …'

The 1884 entry states: 'Sept 17 1884. The clock was satisfactorily wound at 9.45 p.m. by Robert Walpole Esqe L.E. Bligh Esqe and by Lord and Lady Mostyn for the first time after their arrival at Mostyn Hall'.

The Queen of Romania, Elisabeth (alias Carmen Taylor), is listed as being allowed to wind up the clock on 10 September 1890.

On 13 August 1939, the winding was carried out and recorded in the book by Princess Alice Mary of Athlone, only daughter of Queen Victoria's fourth son, HRH Prince Leopold Charles Edward George Albert, 1st Duke of Albany.

It was not always the great and good who took part in the winding; the butler and housekeeper also took part, and on 17 March 1981 Lord Mostyn, Bob Wilkins, the second woodman, and the odd-job man, Alan Ingleson, carried out the winding together.

Subsequent windings, at what is described as the 'Mostyn Winding Party', have been carried out by, amongst others: the Duke and Duchess of Gloucester (2007); Baroness Thatcher (2010): Kate de Rothschild (various) and, to come full circle, Gregory Philip Roger Mostyn, 7th Baron Mostyn.

So, the next time you are in London, have a look at the clock in the Sir Harry and Lady Djanogly Gallery of Clocks and Watches at the British Museum. (Also, don't forget to visit the Mold Gold Cape.)

TITHE WARS

The payment of tithes (originally one tenth of agricultural produce, but later commuted to monetary payments) has its roots in biblical times. The Commutation of Tithe Act of 1836 made this monetary payment the norm, and maps and associated apportionments were produced, copies of which can be found in Mold Library and the Flintshire Record Office at Hawarden.

The payment of tithes in England and Wales were intended to support the Anglican Church, but in many cases tithes had been appropriated by laymen and non-Church bodies. The Methodist revival in the nineteenth century saw a major growth in Nonconformity worship, and by the middle of the century it was estimated that over 75 per cent of the population worshipped in Baptist, Calvinistic Methodist, Wesleyan, Independent or Unitarian chapels and churches. The payment of the tithe became even more of a disputed tax. Welsh people did not see why they should finance what was seen by many as a 'foreign' church only supported by the landowning local gentry.

A leading opponent of payment of the tithe was Thomas Gee, the owner of the Denbigh-based Welsh language newspaper *Baner ac Amserau Cymru*. The other anti-established church movement, amongst whose leaders was David Lloyd George, was the campaign for the Anglican Church in Wales to be disestablished. Clergy were pressurised into giving discounts on the tithe, particularly to the hard-pressed farming communities. In some cases discounts were agreed, but where clergy refused to offer a concession on what they saw as their right, direct action was called for. Feelings ran very high, and the report of a meeting held in Whitford in December 1886 highlights these feelings:

> This Christmastide the season of 'glad tidings of great joy', the English establishment presented itself to the God-fearing Welsh nonconformist peasants in the form of a gang of emergency men – the scum of ruffianism – armed with new regulation police batons. Welsh bailiffs, Welsh auctioneers, Welsh solicitors, refused to outrage their countryman's feelings and opinions by lending themselves to the Ecclesiastical Commissioners and extortionate clerics.

Meetings were held across the county and, in January 1888, the local newspapers reported that the tithe payers of the parishes of Mold, Nerquis and Tryddyn were meeting at the Star Hotel in Mold to agree the best course of action. Anticipating trouble, it was reported in February that the tithe bailiffs and emergency men made their first appearance, being armed with cutlasses, batons and pistols, whilst in May the supporting 9th Lancers are listed as going into camp at Abergele.

The direct action by the tithe payers took several forms, with them initially refusing to pay the tithe, which in turn resulted in distraining orders being issued against them. These orders allowed bailiffs to seize livestock or property to sell to cover payment of the tithe. The distraining parties were in some cases met with passive resistance, but in others there was a considerable amount of violence, thereby preventing goods being seized. The newspapers of the time listed distraints being made at Caergwrle, Nerquis, Tryddyn, Carmel, Whitford, Flint and Holywell, some of which were accompanied by delaying tactics and violence against the distraining parties.

On 20 December 1886 the auctioneer, bailiffs and a police escort arrived in Whitford to seize the property of four farmers who had failed to pay the tithe. One farmer was having two bullocks and a heifer seized, whilst the other three were having stacks of hay confiscated. Tegwyn Thomas takes up the story:

> But it wasn't quite so simple. There had been a blinding snowstorm seven days previously. The bailiffs and the auctioneer were surrounded by some eighty policemen, and a crowd of up to fifteen hundred people protested, with the aiming and throwing of snowballs. The brown felt hat of the auctioneer was rendered shapeless by the onslaught, and he assumed the appearance of a rather disgruntled snowman.

One local distraining agent and auctioneer for the Ecclesiastical Commissioners was Mr A.E. Craft of Nannerch and Mold, for which he was paid 3 guineas a day. Compared to events in Denbighshire, Flintshire protests were relatively quiet, damage to property was negligible and there was only one conviction for assault related to the disturbances. In 1891, the Tithe Act was passed and this transferred the responsibility for paying tithes from the tenant to the landlord. As a result, landlords built the charge into the rent, and failure to pay could therefore result in the tenant being evicted from his property. The payment of tithes continued until 1936, even though the Anglican Church in Wales was disestablished in the 1920s.

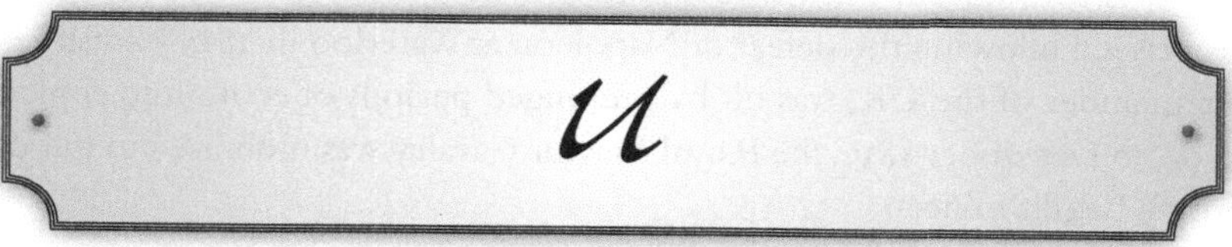

UNREST AND THE FIRST MINERS' UNION

So silent now this place once filled with noise,
Belching chimneys now removed
No more clog shod boys,
Docks and lead works now the distant past
Plundered coal seams costing blood,
Like the Miners, did not last.
Riches made by heartless owners, who
With pittance, hardship, they called pay
To the men who went to hew.

Bagillt Harbour. (David Rowe)

The poem by the late Vince Jones entitled 'Bagillt' is also relevant to other villages and towns throughout Flintshire connected with mining and other industrial enterprises. Following the defeat of Napoleon at Waterloo in 1815 Flintshire, like the remainder of the UK, was hit by prolonged periods of economic depression and, on 10 December 1819, the Royal Maylor Cavalry was mobilised to put down a riot by Bagillt miners.

The miners were seeking a pay increase to compensate for the increase in the cost of living and as a protest against unemployed colliers from Brymbo seeking work. The Friendly Association Coal Miners' Union Society was first established in Lancashire in 1830, and it soon developed a reputation for being militant. The union quickly expanded, and in November 1830 the first branch in Flintshire was established at the Boot Tavern, Bagillt. Whilst details of the leaders of the branch are unknown, they appear to have been very active, as strikes took place throughout the county. Leeswood Hall, the home of the prominent Wynne-Eyton family, and on whose estate there were a number of collieries, was surrounded by local striking miners and brickmakers, making various demands.

In 1831, the Miners' Arms, High Street, Mold, was a meeting place and headquarters of the union for local miners. Striking miners from Mold's Bromfield Colliery rounded up strike-breakers, many of whom were unemployed copper miners from Anglesey, and made them go to the colliery office to be paid off. They then took strike-breakers to the Miners' Arms, where each of the Anglesey men was given 18*s* journey money from union funds. All the strike-breakers were then forcibly marched along the turnpike road to Flint.

The local strike-breakers were allowed to return to Mold, providing they wore their coats inside out, thereby showing that they were strike-breakers. The Anglesey men were taken on to Bagillt, where they could get a ship back home. The leaders of the strike were eventually arrested and brought before the Flintshire Assizes, where a guilty verdict could have resulted in them being transported. Despite the judge instructing the jury that the men were guilty, the members of the jury on this occasion decided to ignore these instructions and returned a not guilty verdict.

During 1844, strikes by miners continued across Flintshire, and it was reported that in January and February striking miners had rioted in Mold, Northop, Greenfield, Holywell and Hawarden.

The above examples highlight the tension existing across the county, and violence during these disturbances was commonplace, in many cases requiring the intervention of the military to restore order. Examination of nineteenth-century census returns for Flintshire shows that the majority of the male workforce were employed in mining and quarrying.

Friedrich Engels, in his book *The Conditions of the Working Class in England*, describes the early start to working life and conditions of many miners, and the following two extracts from the *Children's Employment Commission 1842 Report* by

H. Herbert Jones, on the 'Employment of Children and Young Persons in Mines and Mineral Works in North Wales' paints a graphic picture of life for many families. The section on Coed Talon and Leeswood Coal and Iron Works records children as young as 7 or 8, through family necessity, working twelve-hour days underground and having a limited education. Many of them were not employed directly by the company but by charter masters. One 13 year old was paid *1s 2d* a day, but only part was paid in cash; the remainder was paid in the form of credit at the local 'Tommy' or 'Truck' shop. The Clerk to the Justices expressed his concern about this particular method of paying wages by making the following statement:

> The Chartermasters receive their money in full from the managers. The men and boys whom they employ are in many instances obliged to meet the Chartermasters at a public house, where a great deal of money is spent. The public houses they frequent are often of the lowest order and, the settlement being on a Saturday night, it is not an uncommon thing for some of the men to remain all night, and even all Sunday, in these houses, where the greater part of the wages are consumed, to the great detriment of families.

At the same hearing the Reverend Owen Jones, a Mold Calvinistic minister, also made mention of the life of colliers:

> They live in houses built adjoining each other near the pits, and when work is over they congregate and drink, and smoke, use bad language, and often quarrel. The children suffer by bad example and improvement of the mind cannot take place …

This clearly had an effect not only on their social attitudes, but also their health, and the report went on to detail that 'at 30 a miner begins to look wan and emaciated, and so does a collier at 40 …' and concludes that 'few colliers arrive at the age of 60, and still fewer miners … Bronchial affections attack both miners and colliers, to which disease they sooner or later fall martyrs.'

Three local magistrates, including Mr Wynne-Eyton, were asked for their comments, and their response highlights even further the huge gap between the local landowners and the mining community: 'The miners and colliers live at a distance from them, and they professed to know but little of their habits and customs.' H. Kenneth Birch, in his book *The History of Policing in North Wales*, when referring to the 1869 Mold Riots in which four people were killed, concluded that the experience in Flintshire was a salutary lesson for the rest of the forces in North Wales. Any confrontation with miners meant that the police were faced with a group that was noted for being difficult to handle. Colliers, on the whole, lived a life apart, and from the earliest times had developed a camaraderie and an attitude of defiance to unwelcome authority. As events during the miners' strikes of the 1970s and 1980s only too clearly demonstrated, this practice of mutual support remained unchanged.

UNIVERSITY LINKS WITH FLINTSHIRE

Around the time of the formation of the first Miners' Union in Bagillt, a young man was making his living as a cockle gatherer on the River Dee, probably without any great expectations as to his future. Enoch Robert Gibbon Salisbury, later described as 'sharp and talented', was born in Bagillt on 7 November 1819, to what were said to be 'poor parents'. His abilities were recognised by a Liverpool businessman, Philip Henry Bentham, who found the young Enoch employment in Liverpool.

Not one to waste a golden opportunity, Enoch furthered his limited education at the local Mechanics' Institute, and subsequently he was appointed manager of the Chester United Gas Company. After the various gas companies in Chester were amalgamated, he sought employment in London and worked for the *Daily Post* and *Art Journal*. Whilst working in London, he also took the opportunity to enrol as a law student of the Inner Temple, and in 1852 he was called to the Bar. He subsequently developed a reputation as a parliamentary counsel but also practiced on the North Wales circuit.

A Congregationalist by religious conviction, he also embraced the temperance movement and although a fluent Welsh speaker, he is recorded as giving an address to a temperance meeting in English, whilst other speakers delivered theirs in Welsh. In 1857, he was appointed as one of the two Members of Parliament for Chester under the Liberal flag, the other elected member being Hugh Lupus, Earl Grosvenor.

However, his stay in Parliament was short-lived and he failed to get re-elected in 1859. In 1868 he again failed to obtain a seat, the two seats going to Earl Grosvenor and Henry Cecil Raikes, who lived at Llwynegrin Hall, Mold. The current Flintshire County Council offices and Law Courts are on Raikes Lane.

Prior to the elections, Salisbury portrayed himself as a champion of the people and would often address what were described as 'working men's meetings'. Special verses to a song called 'Cheer Boys Cheers' were written to support his candidacy. These new verses included:

Our old British Nation
With peace and with plenty shall ever flow;
To take away from us our heavy taxation
Electors vote for Salisbury when to the polls you go.

Enoch Gibbon Salisbury beckons us forward
Cheerfully to his aid we will go
And we will gain a glorious victory
If we take heed as to the poll we go.

Although the original version was written by the English composer Henry Russell, the song was adopted by the Confederates during the American Civil War.

During the years 1857–1863, Enoch had a house built (Glan Aber, in the English part of Saltney), and was elected as a member of Chester Council, serving as a magistrate. He was re-elected to the council for the Trinity Ward on a number of occasions, and in his obituary he was described as a 'patriotic Welshman and was immensely popular in Chester'. However, he appeared to provoke displeasure from some electors, as demonstrated by the following extracts from local newspapers: 'one characteristic of the self sufficient political charlatan. One more remarkable for arrogant presumption and dictatorial declamation it was never our painful duty to listen to …', 'the defeat of Mr Enoch Gibbon Salisbury was the crowning triumph of the day. The hypocrisy of this man is almost unbelievable.'

In 1868, a correspondent going under the nom de plume 'Auld Reekie' (the colloquial name for Edinburgh) attacked 'his dictatorial manner', and other critics referred in a derogatory manner to his initial employment as a cockle gatherer. In 1881, he was found guilty by the Chester Election Commissioners of 'guilty and corrupt practices' (bribery) whilst supporting a Liberal candidate. His Liberal friends rallied round him and, following a collection, he was presented with a testimonial and a cheque for £231.

Although a Liberal for many years, he was described as 'turning Unionist in 1886', and this coincided with what was described 'as a reverse of fortune'. Following the death of his wife, he retired to London and died on 27 October 1890 at the Westminster Palace Hotel, where he was living. His body was brought back to Chester and he is buried next to his wife at Eccleston. However, he left an enduring legacy in the form of his library. During his lifetime he was a committed bibliophile and accumulated a collection of approximately 13,000 books as well as maps and prints. Due to his 'reverse of fortune', he sold his collection to the University of South Wales and Monmouth, and this collection, along with later additions, is contained in the Salisbury Rare Books Collection in the University of Cardiff Library.

Whilst we will never know what the real Enoch Salisbury was like, we have to admire the dedication and hard work of the Bagillt 'cockle gatherer'.

The second link related to universities left us an even greater legacy, that of a university founded by the son of a Holywell-born merchant. Perhaps the first thing that comes to mind when you hear the name is to think of the now liquidated, Liverpool-based department store, Owen Owens. Well, our subject is a different Owen Owens.

Born in Holywell, in 1764, he had established a small company before moving to Manchester sometime in the late 1780s. His son John, who was born in 1790, joined the business and it was renamed Owen Owens & Son. Under John's influence the company expanded, and whilst it initially dealt in hat linings, trimmings and manufactured umbrellas, it gradually increased its range. The company became a major exporter and its markets included China, India and North and South America.

By the mid-1840s, world affairs resulted in a major downturn in business, so Owen Owens & Son turned to more speculative ventures whilst at the same time maintaining their personal wealth. Investments in the burgeoning railway companies was a particularly lucrative business activity.

Owen died in 1844 and John only lived for a further two years, dying on 29 July 1846 at the comparatively young age of 55. John had not always enjoyed the best of health, he was a private person and never married, but one of his abiding interests from a young age was that of education. Without an heir, he had offered his fortune to an old school friend, with whom he had a business partnership, but the friend suggested he should found a college in Manchester reflecting John's strong principles and to be free of religious teaching. After bequests to relatives, friends, charities and servants, the residue of his estate, some £100,000 was, under the supervision of trustees, to be used:

> … for the foundation of an institution within the parliamentary borough of Manchester … for providing or aiding the means of instructing and improving young persons of the male sex (and being of an age not less than fourteen years) in such branches of learning or science as are now and may be hereafter usually taught in the English Universities, but subject, nevertheless, to the fundamental and immutable rule and condition that the students, professors, teachers and other officers and persons connected with the said institution shall not make any declaration as to, or submit to any test whatsoever of, their religious opinions …

The college was also to be open to all and without any consideration being given to the applicant's place of birth, rank or condition in society. The trustees proceeded with his instructions, and in 1850 a principal and two professors were appointed. Owens College was formally opened in October 1851 with between eighteen and twenty students.

The college prospered and in 1903 it, along with a number of other independent colleges, was amalgamated to make what we know today as the University of Manchester. The Owens archive is held at the university's John Rylands Library. From relatively humble beginnings in Holywell, the family had a significant influence on higher education, and they would be overjoyed that their foresight resulted in the university being rated third, below Oxford and Cambridge, in terms of 'research power'.

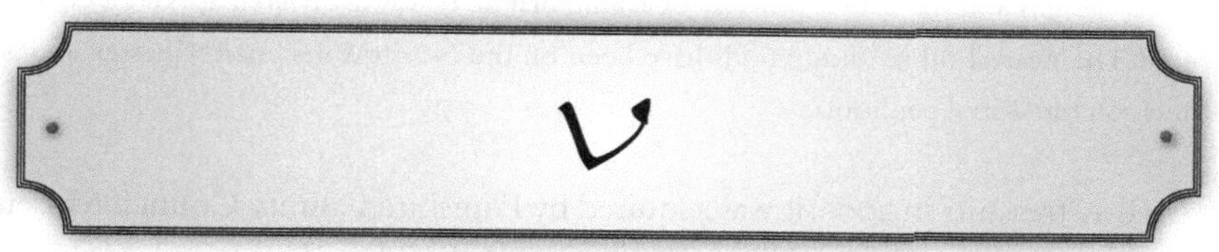

VIKINGS IN FLINTSHIRE

We know from historical records that the Vikings were very active throughout the United Kingdom, and the enduring impression of them as wild and brutal has continued through the intervening centuries. Whilst this is undoubtedly true of many of the groups, we also know that they settled and established communities. Archaeological evidence shows they were also farmers and skilled craftsman, and a visit to the Jorvik Viking Centre in York will reward the visitor who wants to learn more about these people.

We also tend to forget that amongst their descendants were the Normans, who subsequently conquered and transformed Britain. Whilst there is no real evidence for the establishment of permanent Viking settlements in Flintshire, we do have evidence of their presence. In the AD 850s, Vikings from Ireland, the Isle of Man and further afield raided Anglesey and Gwynedd and subsequently settled in Chester. The town was known to have had a large Scandinavian community, and today this is evidenced from the existence of St Olav's church (now redundant) in Lower Bridge Street. Named after a former King of Norway slain in battle, Olav is also the patron saint of Norway.

Huts excavated in Lower Bridge Street were interpreted as of the bow-sided type especially associated with Scandinavian sites in England, and what was perhaps the name of a gate in the city wall in that quarter, Clippe Gate, may well have derived from the Old Norse personal name *Klippr*.

Much of the major Viking activity in North Wales appears to have been centred on Anglesey, although the names of the Great Orme and the Little Orme at Llandudno are derived from Old Norse. Part of the Great Orme is known as Orme's Head and is possibly from the Old Norse '*Orms ætt*' (meaning Orme's family or clan) and likewise, Orme's Bay may be a corruption of Ormesby, the Old Norse '*by*' means farm or enclosure.

The River Dee will certainly have been on the Vikings' extensive trading routes, and a number of significant finds in Flintshire would appear to confirm a definite link. In 2004, a gold ring, 1.9cm in diameter, was discovered by a metal detectorist near Nercwys Hall, and it is described thus:

> It is decorated with wide, shallow facets created by hammering. This decoration is similar to Viking designs and the ring is possibly of Viking origin. It was discovered at Nercwys, near Mold. The nearest other Viking finds have been on the North Wales coast, Chester, and at Meols on the Wirral peninsula.

Declared as 'treasure' in 2006, it was acquired by Flintshire County Council Museums Service and can be seen in the library and museum building, Earl Road, Mold.

The Maen Achwynfan Cross, described in a previous section, is also believed to have a link with the Vikings.

Perhaps the most significant discovery was at the coast near Tan Lan, at Talacre. Archaeological excavation has not uncovered any richly accompanied Viking graves like those found in other parts of Britain and Ireland, but a grave discovered in the early 1930s is described as a simple burial. The grave had been uncovered whilst excavation work was being carried out for a cesspit in connection with the building of a new house.

The cist (stone slab tomb) had overall dimensions of 6ft 6in long by 2ft wide, had no bottom, and the side slabs were embedded into the natural shingle at the base. When the bones were first uncovered, the police were notified and they dug out the interior of the grave to identify any possible evidence that might have

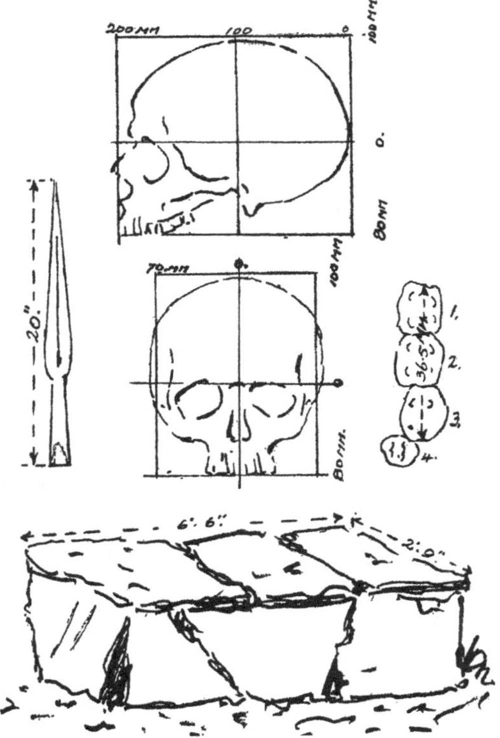

Viking grave. (Llandudno, Colwyn Bay & District Field Club)

been required by the authorities. The skeleton was complete and lying on its back, and detailed measurements were taken and exact scale drawings of the skull and femur were made. These drawings, along with a description of the site were then sent to the Scottish anatomist and anthropologist Sir Arthur Keith who, after investigation, gave the following response:

> Yours is a fine fellow with rather a more pronounced nose than is usual, but otherwise a typical Viking – a man of from 35 to 40 years of age, 5ft 6ins or 5ft 7ins in height with a set of teeth that makes us *moderns* envious. The extra molar in the lower jaw is not common – perhaps one in a hundred or thereabouts. I expect he was a sea Rover – not head of a settled community.

The report of a visit by the Llandudno, Colwyn Bay & District Field Club, states that the remains were to be handed over to Sir Arthur Keith at the Royal College of Surgeons. Upon checking with the Royal College, they advised that the skeleton is not in their possession, so the mystery is – where has he disappeared to?

The assumption that this was a sea rover, and not a leader, was also based on the fact that the only grave goods found were a 20in long iron spearhead and a knife. Various theories were put forward as to the cause of his death, but nothing conclusive was established. So the mystery remains about this unknown ordinary Viking who was buried, as was the custom of the roving bands, in a simple stone cist, facing north-easterly, and close to the sea.

VISITORS AND VACATIONERS AT TIN TOWN

A millennium after the Vikings visited our area, the A55 trunk road provides a direct route to Snowdonia and Holyhead, and so effectively bypasses all the attractions of Flintshire. However, this was not always the case. The area was popular with pilgrims visiting St Winefride's Well at Holywell and in the seventeenth, eighteenth and nineteenth centuries gentrified travellers were recording their visits in published journals.

Flint, so often the butt of scathing comments, attracted many visitors and the *Cambrian Mirror*, in 1851, highlighted its attractions:

> The air is salubrious and the surrounding scenery beautiful. Visitors are well catered for. The walks in the neighbourhood, with the billowing cornfields, are invigorating. A pleasant sail of twelve miles from Chester to Flint might be had for the sum of sixpence ... A great number of Cestrians avail themselves of this opportunity to take their families to Flint during the bathing season. Lodgings and other accommodation may be had at very reasonable rates and visitors are provided at the shortest notice with every requisite accommodation. Hot and cold baths have been constructed on an extensive scale ...

The development of the railways in the nineteenth century saw a further influx of visitors into the area. Later, cheap day returns allowed Mancunians and Scousers to enjoy the attractions of places such as Caergwrle, Hawarden, Holywell and Flint, at a reasonable price. A 'Walking Tour' ticket from Liverpool to Caergwrle Castle would cost 5*s* 7*d* first class, and 3*s* 5*d* third class, but strangely no second class is listed.

We are all conscious of the many caravan sites that populate the coastline, but the provision of second homes started much earlier in Pantymwyn, which ultimately became known as 'Tin Town'. Pantymwyn was well known to Merseysiders before the war because there was a direct bus service from Birkenhead.

There were at least three cafés in Pantymwyn (the Windmill near the bus terminus, Half Way House on Trial Hill and Mrs Reason's in Cefn Bychan Woods) all of which catered for day trippers. Some people built chalets for weekend use or retirement, while others had caravans or wooden cabins for summer visits.

During the Second World War, the bombing of Liverpool and the opening of a large munitions factory at Rhydymwyn led to an increase in demand for temporary dwellings in Pantymwyn. Wallasey County Borough Council also made the decision to remove a number of temporary structures from the foreshore at Moreton-on-the-Wirral, and some of these structures found their way to Pantymwyn Woods. Chalet-type structures appeared along the Cefn Bychan and Pen-y-Fron roads. In most instances, these have now been replaced by permanent houses.

'Empire Pride' – des res. (Dr Malcolm Seaborne)

One house, 'Annville', was listed as having been built using packing cases from Liverpool Docks, and pictured is a house named as 'Empire Pride'. Amongst the other house names were 'Glenholme', 'Cefn Bryn', 'Lynwood' and 'Norwood'.

Local people also needed their vacations, and Rhyl and Llandudno were popular destinations for Flintshire people. The *North Wales Chronicle* published a weekly article entitled 'The Rhyl Visitor', and this listed the bathing hours and tide table, along with a list of visitors and where they were staying. In September 1850, Mr and Mrs Lambe and family, of Celyn, Caergwrle, stayed at Mrs Spencer's in Sea Street, while Mrs Harrison and Mrs Jones were staying at Woodland Cottage, Quay Street. Two years later, in July 1852, the Reverend and Mrs Williams and family of Nannerch were staying at the same Woodland Cottage.

As most people are aware, Llandudno remains relatively unchanged, and in 1890 William Gillespie of Plas Isa, Llong, clearly made his feelings known about the proposal to build a pier in the centre of Llandudno Bay. He wrote to the *North Wales Chronicle* stating his objections:

> ... A needless structure – an eyesore and a great obstruction ... If erected, the bay would be completely spoiled and one of the greatest attractions of the town would cease to exist. The egress and ingress of visitors would be of a different class of people, and in that case Llandudno would become a third rate watering place.

Clearly he did *not* want the town to be accessible to all!

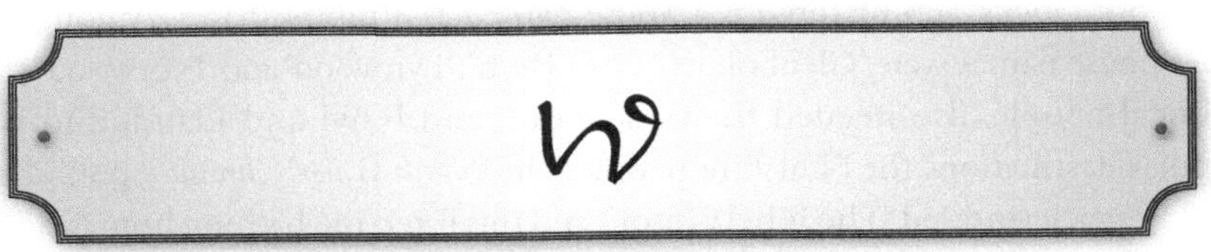

WARS

Crimean and Boer

Throughout the centuries, Flintshire has provided many personnel and has several stories related to wars. The 5th Battalion (Flintshire) of the Royal Welch Fusiliers (RWF) saw active service throughout the First World War, including action at Suvla Bay, where they suffered many casualties and deaths. (When referring to the RWF the archaic spelling 'Welch' has been used in the regimental title, although it should be noted that from the late nineteenth century until the early 1920s the spelling 'Welsh' was used.)

The Crimean War (1854–56), did not rank amongst the greatest campaigns of the British Army, and one particular action is recorded in poetry:

> Theirs not to reason why,
> Theirs but to do and die:
> Into the valley of Death
> Rode the six hundred.

The extract from Alfred, Lord Tennyson's famous poem 'The Charge of the Light Brigade' tells the tale of the infamous major military blunder during the Crimean War. During the Battle of Balaclava, only 140 of the 637 officers and men of the Light Brigade who took part in the fatal charge returned.

All the survivors suffered wounds of some nature, but many continued with their military service and one, Kilkenny-born Troop Sergeant Major Thomas Ryan of Shotton, lived to the ripe old age of 88 years. At the end of his military service he returned to live with his son and family at No. 23 Wellington Street, Shotton. In late 1908, he left his home to visit friends in Connah's Quay but never returned, and it was two months later when his body was found in the River Dee. He was laid to rest, with full military honours, in St Deiniol's churchyard, on 19 December 1908.

Over the years, his local Tinkersdale sandstone memorial deteriorated, and the writing was becoming illegible until in 2001 Hawarden Community Council and others arranged for the replacement and rededication of the memorial tablet. The grave is signposted at the rear of St Deiniol's church. His obituary referred to him as serving with the 4th Light Dragoons, before being seconded as Troop Sergeant Major of the 17th Lancers at Balaclava. His headstone contains the following inscription:

> I have fought the good fight, Alma, Inkerman, Balaclava, Sevastopol. Thomas Ryan, a native of Kilkenny and late Troop Sergeant Major in HM XVII Lancers. Whom God's High Grace saved from death in the memorable Light Cavalry Charge at Balaclava and during the perils of the Crimean Campaign, took his final discharge on 20 October 1908 aged 88 years.

Unfortunately it was not possible to verify the accuracy of this story with the 17th Lancers Regimental Museum, but research (including correspondence from Ryan's troop commander) carried out by a previous county archivist, indicates that the story is true, and the museum's records are being amended accordingly. Following Ryan's death, his troop commander, Captain Godfrey Morgan (later Viscount Tredegar), wrote the following letter to a local paper:

> I am much obliged for your letter, dated 20 December 1908, informing me of the recovery of the body of Thomas Ryan, late of the 17th Lancers, and of his burial with military honours yesterday, and of the sad intelligence that he had been missing for so long. I shall be pleased to receive any information you possess as to the position of his son at the present time.

Lord Tredegar, who is buried in Monmouthshire, is believed to be the only other burial in Wales of a participant in the fatal charge. However, the grave of another participant in the battle can be found across the border in Knutsford churchyard. The grave is that of Trumpet Major William Smith who, after more than twenty-five years of service in the regular army, joined the still very much active Cheshire Yeomanry.

In October 2013, the bugle that sounded the fatal charge appeared on an edition of the *Antiques Roadshow*. Lord Cardigan's trumpeter, Private William Brittain, was fatally wounded and following his death the bugle was given to his family. It was brought onto the show by Captain Nick Holtby of the Queens Royal Lancers and Nottinghamshire Yeomanry Museum.

In the same year as Thomas Ryan's death, another local survivor of the Crimean War – Charles Owen, of Garden Place, Mold, aged 77 – was given a full military funeral at the English Presbyterian church and is buried in Mold cemetery.

In St James' cemetery, Holywell, will be found a memorial to a local soldier killed in the Crimean War, Sergeant Edwards, of the 23rd Regiment (Royal Welch Fusiliers).

The second Boer War (1899–1902) once again involved Welsh soldiers, and Captain Thomas Mann Keene, of the Mold solicitors, Keene & Kelly, was given command of the 1st Volunteer Active Service Company, comprising

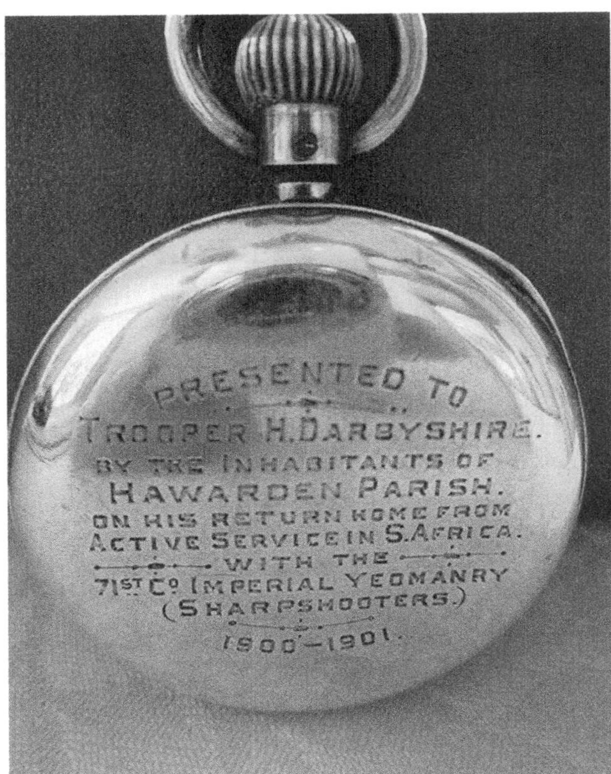

Henry Darbyshire's presentation watch. (Susan Phillips)

officers and men drawn from the 1st, 2nd and 3rd Volunteer Battalions of the Royal Welch Fusiliers. To prove nothing much changes with respect to the supply of equipment, a public subscription fund was organised and from the money raised he was given a revolver and a pair of field glasses.

One individual from Hawarden, a member of the Cheshire Yeomanry, Henry Darbyshire, enlisted in 1900 in the Imperial Yeomanry Sharpshooters and was allowed to defer the last year of his apprenticeship at Sandycroft Foundry. Henry, whose father-in-law was Inspector Conquest of Scotland Yard, received, as we detailed earlier, a Bible from the rector of Hawarden, Reverend Stephen Gladstone. On his return, a public subscription fund was raised and he was presented with a pocket watch by Lady Cavendish.

The Second World War and the POW Artist

Amongst the many tragedies and hardships for British troops during the Second World War, one particular event has been made into a number of films including *The Bridge over the River Kwai* in 1957, and in 2013's *The Railway Man*. These tell of the suffering of the troops who were involved in the building of the Burma–Thailand Railway (the 'Death Railway').

One such soldier was the late Hugh Thomas Owen who was born in a cottage in Alyn Row, Pontblyddyn, in 1918. Educated at Pontblyddyn School, he left aged 14 and had various jobs before receiving his military call-up, in 1939.

His initial training was carried out at the Royal Welch Fusiliers' Hightown Barracks, Wrexham, followed by a cook's course in Lincoln and then a posting to a camp just outside Barnard Castle in County Durham. Afterwards he was posted overseas, and whilst en route to Nova Scotia was diverted via Capetown to Singapore, arriving on 11 January 1942. Following three weeks of action against the Japanese, he was taken prisoner on 15 February 1942, and initially was required to work on clearing away the debris in Singapore.

Towards the end of 1942, the prisoners of war were transported on a 1,000-mile train journey to Bangkok. The journey took five days and nights, and during this, they received only one meal of 'dirty rice'. As the wagons had no sanitary provision, cholera became rife. On arrival at Bangkok, they were marched through the jungle for over four weeks, travelling the 300 miles at night to avoid reconnaissance planes. They laid low during the day, with the dying left where they lay, until they reached Railway Camp 5 at Song Kalia.

Initially, Hugh worked in the hospital caring for cholera patients, but after about six months he was transferred to a working party on the railway, where he remained for approximately twelve months. Over 1,600 men died at this camp and only twenty-five survivors were transferred back to Changi Gaol in Singapore. For the next six months he worked on the building of an aerodrome runway. During his period of imprisonment the basic fayre had been dirty rice with maggots, and the

New RWF recruit, aged 21. (Hughie Owen)

slice of bread they were given by the ATS on liberation was the first the prisoners had seen for four years. He only weighed 5 stone on his return to Wales, and even in his 80s the memory of those days brought tears to his eyes.

However, despite the deprivations whilst he was a POW, the human spirit still finds a way to express itself. Hugh was a gifted artist, and when he was on the outside working parties at Changi, he memorised, bit by bit, the structure of the prison building. On return to his ground-floor cell, he sketched the prison on a small piece of cardboard with a stump of a pencil sharpened on the concrete floor. The drawing took a considerable length of time, and if it had been discovered he would have been severely punished or even killed. His interest in art continued throughout his life, and his house was full of his own paintings. A remarkable man that it was a privilege to know.

Grange Cavern and German Dams

Opening in 1979, the 2½-acre Grange Cavern Military Museum housed a large collection of old military vehicles, weaponry, ordnance, badges, buttons and medals in the old mine workings some 20–30m below the surface. The galleries had been created by the quarrying of limestone by hand in the early nineteenth century. The stone was transported on a tramway system known as 'Crockford's Way' which extended from Pantasaph to Greenfield Dock via the Grange Cavern. It was then taken by sea to its ultimate destination, including the construction of the south Liverpool docks.

Grange Cavern Museum. (David Rowe)

In the Second World War it was taken over by the Ministry of Defence and used to house bombs, including, it is claimed, the famous 'Bouncing Bombs'. Designed by Barnes Wallis, they were used in the raids on the Möhne, Eder and Sorpe dams, as part of Operation Chastise carried out by 617 Squadron of Lancaster bombers. The operation was detailed in two books: *The Dam Busters* by Paul Brickhill, and *Enemy Coast Ahead* by the leader of the raid, Wing Commander Guy Gibson. In 1954–55, a movie called *The Dam Busters* was released to commemorate the raid, and the accompanying march, composed by Eric Coates, still features in today's military parades. Unfortunately, the accuracy of this particular story has never been established. Is it likely that the bombs for the Lincolnshire-based 617 Squadron would be stored so far away?

Sadly the museum only remained open until 1989, and after closure the remarkable and important collection was scattered far and wide and the doors locked on the empty caverns.

❧ WELLS ❧

Holy and Cursing, and the 'Nowt of Holywell

> Pistyll Rhaeadr and Wrexham Steeple
> Snowdon's Mountain with its people
> Overton Yew trees, Gresford bells,
> Llangollen Bridge and St Winefride's well.

Listed as one of the seven wonders of Wales, St Winefride's Well has many tales associated with its healing properties, and has been described by some as the 'Lourdes of Wales'.

As well as the many healing miracles attributed to St Winefride, it is claimed that in 1119 she assisted Richard d'Avranches, son of the Hugh Lupus, 1st Earl of Chester. Richard had been making a pilgrimage to the well when he was attacked by the Welsh and was forced to take refuge in Basingwerk Abbey. He prayed for his saint to intervene, and it is claimed that she caused a sandbank to form across the Dee Estuary, allowing the Constable of Chester to bring a rescue force across. Local legend has it that the location hereafter was known as 'Constable Sand'. However, Richard's guardian was sadly missing in 1120, when both he and his wife, Matilda of Blois, died in the White Ship Disaster off Barfleur, Normandy. Also drowned was the heir to the throne of Henry I, William Adelin, thereby setting in motion the succession war between Matilda and Stephen.

The well remains a place of pilgrimage, and is often the first stopping place of many Irish people on their journey from Holyhead to destinations in England.

Needless to say the well has also attracted 'characters', and one such person had as many differing character descriptions as aliases. Born Frederick William Rolfe on 22 July 1860, he was also known as 'Baron Corvo' (he claimed he owed the title to an elderly English lady, the Duchess Sforza-Cesarini, who more or less adopted him as a grandson and bestowed on him a small estate with a baronial title, but there is no evidence to support this claim), 'Frank English', 'Frederick Austin', 'Prospero', 'Caliban', 'A. Crab Maid' and 'Fr Rolfe'. He was also described in a variety of ways by those who knew him: 'brilliant writer', 'fantasist', 'self-tortured and defeated soul', 'a man of taste with a pleasant turn of the tongue', 'paranoid'.

Dr Hardy, Principal of Jesus College, Oxford, described him as 'a refined and honourable gentleman, whose moral character is without reproach'. Rolfe also received good testimonials from the heads of schools where he taught. Other descriptions included: 'eccentric, vain, poseur, caustic tongue, sense of superiority', 'vaguest sense of realities', 'his life was blameless … no guile in him … innocent as a 3-year-old', 'shy and timid rather than self-assertive and bullying', 'biggest liar we had ever met', 'ruthless selfishness', 'selfish and self-centred', 'genius on the very border', 'an insatiable appetite for gossip … as knowledge is power'.

Rolfe even claimed that the German Kaiser was his godfather. He saw himself as a permanently picturesque figure, oppressed by a circle of enemies jealous of his talents or exhibiting their own meanness, and he is even believed to have forged letters by the owner of the *Holywell Record*, F.W. Hocheimer. Throughout his life, he had arguments and made vitriolic attacks on old friends and people who had helped him; this was later described as 'nature tortured by disappointment that could not be satisfied'.

So who was this complex character? Born in London in 1860, Rolfe left school at the age of 14 and obtained a post as an under-master at Grantham School, where he met and remained a lifelong friend of the headmaster, Dr Hardy. In 1886, he converted to Catholicism and believed he had a vocation for the priesthood. Following a further period of teaching, including at the Marquess of Bute's school for outcast children, he decided to enter the priesthood. As an ecclesiastical subject of the Bishop of Shrewsbury, Rolfe entered Oscott (RC) College in 1887, but only stayed a few months before being discharged.

Temporary tutorships then followed, before the Archbishop of Edinburgh sponsored him for enrolment in the Pontifical Scots College in Rome. His approach and attitude to priests and fellow students, coupled with his lack of any commitment to study, resulted in him being expelled after five months with the scathing comment, 'no vocation'.

On his return to Britain, he appears to have been an art student, photographer and secretary to a Labour leader, Mr Champion. Wherever he went he left debts, and continued to fall out with people who had tried to provide him with support and assistance. In 1895, he sought aid and work from the friars at Pantasaph, but once again found himself unpopular and was ejected due to his argumentative nature and a total disregard for what was required of him.

He next appears at St Winefride's Well after being commissioned to paint processional banners, some of which can still be viewed in the small museum attached to the well. However, he had a major dispute with Fr Beauclerk SJ, who he saw as the main source of his troubles in Holywell, and eventually he managed to have the priest removed from the parish, who then went to Malta for two years as chaplain to the forces.

Corvo banner. (Holywell & District Society)

During his time in Holywell, Rolfe published 'confidences' in the local paper, the *Holywell Record*. Due to the nature of his aggressive and confrontational writing, where he attacked everyone he knew, the paper ultimately went out of business.

Rolfe wrote a short story about his time in Holywell called 'Sewers End', in which he describes himself as the 'Nowt of Holywell', along with scathing remarks about the locals: 'The bumpkins could not bother their beery heads simultaneously with a truth and their own patent romances ...'

In January 1899, we find him applying for admission to the Holywell Workhouse using the name 'Alfred Austin', which just happened to be the name of the Poet Laureate in 1896 – another deception? Later that year he appears to have left Holywell, and after periods in Oxford, Rome and Christchurch, he could be found in Venice in 1907. With his sexual orientation, he sought out the company of young gondoliers, and one of his books, *A Romance of Modern Venice or the Desire and Pursuit of the Whole*, describes his time in Venice, although this was considered libellous by publishers. He remained in Venice until his death, aged 53, on 25 October 1913 and it was only afterwards that his true ability as a writer was fully appreciated.

One critic reviewing *The Chronicles of the House of Borgia* wrote, 'when the mighty family of Borgia is dealt with in the future this volume will be a standard work of reference, but consider him almost as great a problem as the strange family whose fortunes he has traced.' Many of his stories were autobiographical in nature, including one that he wrote for the *Wide World Magazine* which highlights the fantasist in him, called 'How I was buried alive'.

We will never know the true personality of this interesting and complex character, but he has left a legacy in the form of his many published stories.

Returning to wells in general, a dedicated webpage explains the background to and details of the ancient, holy and healing wells of the county: http://wellhopper.wordpress.com/category/county/flintshire.

Unfortunately, not all wells have been used for good, and various court cases outline how wells have been exploited by unscrupulous individuals looking to make money from the more gullible and unwary members of the community. Where this practice was followed, wells became known as 'cursing wells'. If you had a particular grievance against someone, you wrote the person's name on a piece of paper and paid to have it put into the well. To have the name withdrawn, the affected person then paid for its removal, so the person controlling such wells was in a win-win situation.

Whilst it has not been possible to identify any such wells within the current county boundaries, this practice was certainly followed by individuals in Flintshire. In 1820, a Flintshire man was found guilty of defrauding a person from Holywell of 15*s* by telling him that he had been cursed, and pretending to procure the removal of his name from a certain cursing well. Shortly afterwards the man, who had been suffering from an undefined illness, believed he had been cured. A coincidence? I will let you, the reader, decide.

WITCHCRAFT AND THE BUCKLEY PORRINGER

It was not just wells that were used for dastardly practices, and one such tale recounted by the Reverend Eirlys Gruffydd is particularly gruesome.

The Museum of Welsh Antiquities at Bangor houses many strange and wonderful objects. Amongst them is a Buckley earthenware pot (a porringer), measuring about 13cm high and about the same dimension across. It was discovered on 3 October 1871 by a labourer, one Edward Morris, who was employed by the Hon. W.O. Stanley MP. The man was removing an old earthen bank on Penrhos Bradwen Farm, Penrhos, Holyhead, when he found it. Its mouth was covered by a slate on which was scratched (on both sides) in crude letters 'NANNY ROBERTS'. Inside the pot were the bones of a frog, together with its dried skin, which was pierced by about forty pins.

There can be no doubt that this pot and its gruesome contents were used to curse the unfortunate Nanny Roberts. This method of bewitching someone was often practised by witches in nineteenth-century Wales. A live frog was identified with the person to be cursed, pierced with pins, and entombed in the pot. As the frog lingered and died, so did the bewitched person. The curse could only be lifted if the pot was found and the frog released. In the case of Nanny Roberts, this was not the case as the pot had been too well-hidden in the earthen bank. Little did the Buckley potter who made this pipkin realise for what dubious purpose it would be used.

The Nanny Roberts cursing pot. (Gwynedd Museums Service)

⸎ X-SITE – MUSTARD GAS, ATOMIC BOMB, ⸎ THE RUSSIAN SPY AND WELSH BROADCASTS

Situated in a valley on the edge of a picturesque village, much of which was owned by the Davies-Cooke family of Gwysaney, is the site of the former Bryn Celyn lead and zinc mine, a site with not one, but two wartime secrets. The entrance to the Valley Works, Rhydymwyn, will be found on the Nant Alyn Road. In 1939, ICI's Special Product Division was instructed, by the Ministry of Supply, to construct a factory to manufacture and store mustard gas. The plant came into operation in 1940, and whether the location of the site was actually known to the Germans is unclear, but certainly workers kept its true purpose secret even from their own families.

In 1942, early work on the atomic bomb, known by the code name 'Tube Alloys', began in building P6 and was staffed by scientists from the UK and Europe, including the German-born Klaus Fuchs, whose father was a professor of theology. Fuchs attended universities in Germany, Bristol and finally Edinburgh, where he was awarded a Doctorate of Science. Between 1939 and 1940, he is listed as a Carnegie Trust Fund Research Fellow at Edinburgh University, and in 1943 he was elected as a fellow of the Institute of Physics. Fuchs was originally a member of the German Communist party, but with the rise of the Nazi party he emigrated to the United Kingdom in 1933. However, being a German citizen he was classed as an 'alien' and in 1939 he was held in an internment camp in Quebec, Canada.

His skills as a scientist were recognised and he was allowed back to Edinburgh in 1941. In 1942 he signed the Official Secrets Act and, despite his known political affiliations, he became a naturalised British citizen. Around seventy scientists, under the management of another German-born scientist, Rudolph Peierls, with Fuchs as his deputy, started work on the 'Tube Alloys' project.

During Fuchs' relatively short stay at the Valley site, he lived on the outskirts of Mold at Maes Alyn, Denbigh Road. Following the signing of the Quebec Agreement in 1943, which committed future development of the bomb to North America, a number of UK-based scientists moved to the USA. They continued their work on what was known as the 'Manhattan Project'. In 1943, Peierls and Fuchs were transferred to the USA, and worked as consultants for the Kellex Corporation, before moving on to the Manhattan Project in Los Alamos, New Mexico. As early as 1941 it is believed that Fuchs had become a Russian spy and was passing information on to the KGB.

At the end of the war, Fuchs returned to the United Kingdom as head of the Theoretical Physics Division, at the Harwell Energy Research Establishment, whilst continuing to pass on information to the Soviets. The authorities were, at this stage, monitoring his activities and in 1949, he was arrested on espionage charges. After pleading guilty, he was sentenced to fourteen years in prison before being released early in June 1959, whereupon he emigrated to communist East Germany. He continued with his research work, and was appointed deputy director of East Germany's Nuclear Research Institute, before dying in East Berlin on 28 January 1988.

The value of the information he passed on to the Soviets has been the subject of much discussion, as some consider that his work did not advance the progress our former Second World War ally had already made. The discovery of his activities did have a significant effect, however, in that the USA accelerated

Building P6 – Tube Alloys Project. (Colin Barber)

its development programme and, within the course of a few months, both the USSR and the USA confirmed that they possessed an atomic bomb.

Although many of the buildings and specially constructed tunnels still exist at Rhydymwyn, the site now hosts two generally peace-loving organisations: Rhydymwyn Valley History Society and the Rhydymwyn Valley Nature Reserve. Both groups run programmes of events throughout the year so, whether you want to know about a spotted fly-catcher or a spy-catcher, there will be something at the site for you.

It is difficult to know how much espionage was actually carried out in Flintshire during the war years, but the story of one Nercwys-born RAF air gunner, Warrant Officer Raymond Hughes, has been well documented.

After the family moved to Pwllglas in Mold, Raymond was educated at Mold Council School and the Alun School before starting work at Oliver's Boot Stores, High Street, Mold, at the age of 15. From there, he was promoted to manager of the Bangor branch. In 1941, he enlisted in the RAF Volunteer Reserve where, after training as an air gunner, he was posted to 467 Squadron Royal Australian Air Force, part of No 5 Group, Bomber Command. The squadron flew Lancaster heavy bombers, and were initially based at RAF Scampton, Lincolnshire, before being relocated to RAF Bottesford in Lincolnshire. The squadron flew its first mission on 2 January 1943 and was repeatedly in action against targets in France, Germany, Norway, Italy and Czechoslovakia.

By August 1943 Hughes, then 20 years of age with a rank of sergeant, had flown twenty missions, but on the evening of 17 August his luck finally ran out. The squadron took part in the raid on the Germans' Peenemunde Rocket Research Centre, where the V1 flying bomb and V2 rockets were being developed. During the raid, his aircraft was shot down by a German fighter, and the crew of six parachuted out of the plane. Hughes was captured and transported to Durchgangslager der Luftwaffe (known to prisoners as 'Dulag Luft') Interrogation Centre. It was said at his post-war court martial that whilst Hughes was at Dulag Luft he started providing assistance to his captors and this earned him some privileges.

Sometime in 1943, he appeared in Berlin, rented a flat and, using a number of aliases (John Charles Baker, George Becker and Raymond Sharples) started paid work for Radio Metropole and the German Foreign Ministry. A few of his broadcasts were made in Welsh, and it is said that these included the Welsh National Anthem and the Lord's Prayer.

Towards the end of the war Hughes, unknown to him, had been promoted to a warrant officer and was returned to a prisoner of war camp until it was liberated by the Russians in April 1945. However, before being repatriated he was arrested and charged with eleven offences, some of which carried the death penalty. The charges included:

1. Giving the enemy information about RAF methods used on the raids he was shot down on.
2. Aiding the enemy by asking prisoners at Dulag Luft 1 to give Germans information on RAF formations.
3. Making propaganda records.
4. Broadcasting propaganda from Berlin Radio.
5. Lending money to those forming the British Free Corps intended for warlike operations against the Russians.
6. Aiding the enemy on combating raids over Berlin.
7. Accepting employment at Berlin Radio.
8. Accepting employment at the German Foreign Office.

The case was heard at the RAF depot, Uxbridge, Middlesex, where Hughes pleaded not guilty to all the charges, and whilst he was acquitted on six, being found guilty of the others could still have resulted in the application of the death penalty. The pilot of his Lancaster and a number of other witnesses spoke highly of him, and these comments may have influenced the lenient sentence reported in the newspapers of the time:

> Warrant Officer Raymond Davies Hughes, 22-year-old air gunner was sentenced to 5 years penal servitude and discharge with ignominy for helping the Germans whilst a POW. Hughes was the first repatriated prisoner to be charged before the Uxbridge Court Martial, which dealt with certain activities of certain aircrew personnel during captivity.

On appeal, the sentence was reduced to two years and nothing more was heard of Hughes until 1951, when Ivor Wynne Jones, in his book *Hitler's Celtic Echo*, states that Hughes arrived in Mold in a Rolls-Royce, and stopped outside a butcher's shop in Wrexham Street. In the same publication mention is made of Hughes attending a funeral in Nercwys in 1993, but with very few people actually recognising him.

His family always believed he was a double agent, and during his court martial he claimed that during his broadcasts he did detail information related to the bombing raids on Berlin. Sadly, the BBC did not have a Welsh speaker available at these times so his claim could not be verified.

However, he was not totally forgotten, as the Bangor-born Welsh writer and playwright, William Owen Roberts, included the story of Hughes in his play 'Radio Cymru – the story of Hitler's Welshmen'. The no longer existing Dalier Sylw Theatre Company performed the play around Wales in 2000.

YE ANCIENT ORDER OF FROTH BLOWERS AND 'SHOOTING YOUR LINEN'

In the section on the Boer War we were introduced to Henry Darbyshire, and in this tale we meet him again at the family-built and owned Central Hotel in Shotton.

Most people are probably aware of the many sporting and social and benevolent societies, such as the Buffaloes and Shepherds, which used pubs as their headquarters. However, not many will have heard of this particular charitable organisation. Whilst researching local history associated with the Darbyshire family, I came across a single cufflink with the initials 'AO' and a badge bearing the word 'Blaster'. Only having a limited knowledge of what these were related to, a quick search of the web turned up details of the organisation in which Henry Darbyshire, of the Central Hotel, held the position of Blaster.

Furthermore, the site gave details of other branches (or VATs, as they were known) in Flintshire: the Market Vaults in Mold (Blower A. Stott); the Swan in Flint (Blower R. Armstrong); Hawarden Castle, in Flint (Blower E.J. Roberts) and the No 5 Flying School, RAF Sealand (Blower Flight Lieutenant E.H. Hooper).

This worthy body went by the name of the Ancient Order of Froth Blowers (AOFB), and was established as a charitable body in 1924 but sadly went out of existence in the 1930s, although interested parties can still enlist in the Friends of the AOFB.

Life membership of the Froth Blowers cost 5*s* and the privileges of club membership included the use of corkscrews, sawdust, note and other paper, and silver cufflinks, etc. The membership card proudly proclaims that:

> THIS ANCIENT GUILD [*c.* 1924] exists to foster the noble Art and gentle and healthy Pastime of FROTH BLOWING amongst Gentlemen-of-Leisure and Ex-Soldiers. After payment of the Subscription you will be Permitted to blow the froth from your own beer, other members' beer, and occasionally off non-members' beer providing they are not looking or are of peaceful disposition.

The organisation had the following mission statement:

> A sociable and law abiding fraternity of absorptive Britons who sedately consume and quietly enjoy with commendable regularity and frequentation the truly British malted beverage as did their forebears and as Britons ever will, and be damned to all pussyfoot hornswogglers from overseas and including low brows, teetotallers and MPs and not excluding nosey-parkers, mock religious busy bodies and suburban fool hens all of which are structurally solid bone from the chin up.

According to the membership card, membership offered a very special privilege – 'Immunity from Arrest'. The Metropolitan Police had been requested not to arrest or apprehend any person under the influence of drink should he be wearing AOFB cufflinks at the time of the debauch!

Founded by Bert Temple, an ex-soldier, and Sir Alfred Fripp, an eminent surgeon whose patients included the royal family, the primary aim of the organisation was fundraising for children's charities, and in particular Sir Alfred Fripp's 'Wee Waifs Fund' in the East End of London. 'Auto outings for bairns' were arranged by the members, and this was organised by 'Monsoon' Lieutenant Colonel P.C. Saunders.

By 1926 membership was over 370,000, and the charity had received in excess of £70,000 in donations and local charities benefitted by means of the various fines etc., imposed at individual VATs.

The Froth Blowers had established themselves globally, and were particularly popular in army messes across the world, with India hosting many VATs. One of the attractions of the organisation was that it was open to all, men and women, and the youngest recorded member was a 'Master Hunter' of Portsmouth – born on 1 December 1926 at 11.55 p.m., he was registered with the AOFB two hours later at 1.55 a.m.

It is believed that, at its peak, the AOFB had a membership of over 700,000, with the highest membership book number identified as 674,125. This was issued to 'Fairy Belle Katherine Kinney' from New York.

Each VAT comprised of a minimum twenty-five members, and by 1929 there were in excess of 2,350 VATs, with gatherings conducted by the Senior Blower. Blowers were required to memorise the following:

> Qualifications, Privileges and Penalties of his rank.
> He must procure the cash of 25 new members to the A.O.F.B. He must be British and be proud of it. He must always carry a corkscrew. He must always lisp when ordering a 'Bass' so that other A.O.F.B.s may at once recognise his rankness. He must doff his bonnet to all pawnbroker's signs and brewers drays. He will act, if requested, as godfather to any hopper's child, always provided however that the child should be born in the hop field (Kent only) where its father is actually actively employed. It is desirable that the child's mother should also be present. A Blaster must not eat whelks with a steel fork, chew the date off his railway tickets, eat asparagus with boxing gloves on …

The organisation had a variety of ranks awarded for recruiting new members, starting with a Blaster (twenty-five members), then a Tornado (100 members), Monsoon (500 members) and a Grand Typhoon (1,000 members). The special ranks and high-ranking members had wonderful titles including:

> Froth Blower No 1 and Fairy Godfather of the Angelic Order of Fairy Belles.
>
> Welcome Breeze [lady].
>
> Wee Puff [lady].
>
> Grand Hurricane [Editor and owner of *Sporting Times*, which became the mouthpiece of the organisation].
>
> Chief Froth and Meat Carver [Popularised the AOFB in the City of London].
>
> The Grand Overseas Scrounger [The gentlemen concerned was an officer on the RMS *Edinburgh Castle*, which travelled between the United Kingdom and South Africa. He also acted as the AOFB ambassador to South Africa and was a very successful recruiter; over 12,000 members were credited to him].
>
> The Sou'West Gale. [This person's brief was to promote membership throughout the armed forces].

The Froth Blowers had their own anthem called 'The More We Are Together', based on a 1768 traditional Austrian folk song; it has the following chorus:

> The more we are together together together
> The more we are together the merrier we'll be
> For your friends are my friends
> And your friends are my friends
> And the more we are together the merrier we will be.

The movement proved so popular, that Nat Travers performed a song called 'I'm One of the Old Froth Blowers' around the country's music halls.

Harold Stewart Turner (Grand Armourer) was the managing director of the Birmingham Medal Company, and was responsible for much of the manufacture of various products to support the fund. Items included tankards, cigarette cases, match cases, powder compacts and even car and motorcycle mascots. Whilst not normal practice, the company took its social responsibilities very seriously, employing disabled servicemen who had difficulty finding employment elsewhere. In addition to those products manufactured by the Birmingham Medal Company, other items were produced, including pipes, socks, ties, and even toilet and shaving soap. Even your dog could be enrolled in the AOFB (Amiable Order of Faithful Bow-wows), and special hallmarked silver dog collars were produced, along with a set of rules which include the wonderful 'To abstain from blowing the froth off the cat's milk' and 'To refrain from biting holes in Ford cars.'

At meetings of a VAT, a procedure was followed where firstly a chairman and various officers were appointed, including a 'Sub-assistant Vice Gargler'. On the order 'shoot your linen, Blowers', attendees would extend their arms in front of them to expose both their AOFB cufflinks, or in the case of ladies, display their bracelet. Failure to have two links, or not wearing a bracelet would leave the miscreant open to various penalties, including fines, buying a round of drinks, having their beer only served in egg cups, having to sing the AOFB anthem to a complete stranger over the telephone (picked at random from the phone book by the aforesaid Vice Gargler), and in the worst cases, wearing their clothes back to front.

However, there were exceptions as to when cufflinks need not be worn: 'where there is no beer within a 125-mile radius', or 'when undergoing surgical operations, pack drill, competing for lightweight boxing championship, riding the favourite in the Derby'.

Not everyone was welcome at a meeting of VATs, and rule No. 11 stated that 'any communist, murderer, conscientious objector or other vermin attending any meeting to be instantly ejected and a dose of Veramon [laxative] forcibly administered'. The following slogan was adopted by the order:

> LUBRICATION IN MOTION
> The British human motor requires regular and reasonable lubrication and British Beer is the best for British Machines. Hops are the fruits of the earth and are Nature's genuine tribute to the human engine. Spirits are not comparable to Beer, but are useful for tanning leather, coats of stomachs, livers and other vitals. Excessive use of spirits will corrode the works and a moderate use of same is only beneficial to ancient or worn-out engines.

As may be expected, the organisation was not without its critics and some people claimed it encouraged children and young people to drink beer. Questions were asked in the House of Commons, and one major opponent was the American prohibitionist and temperance advocate, William Eugene 'Pussyfoot' Johnson. He was a law enforcement officer who openly admitted to lying, planting evidence and bribery to gain convictions, and claimed to have travelled the world three times, giving over 4,000 lectures against alcohol. During one such speech in Britain, he was heckled by students and unfortunately a missile was thrown and blinded Johnson in one eye. Another opponent of the order was a Bradford Methodist minister, Sam Rowley, whose sermons against the 'evils of drink' used to go on for hours. In response, Bert Temple in his 1926 Christmas address asked members to remember the slogan:

> LUBRICATION IN MODERATION, and thus give old Pussyfoot Johnson, and all his freakish tribe, no opening for foistering his unnatural tastes on our British beer-loving, baccy-loving and beef-loving palates.

Membership Card No. 395622

Name

Address

DO YOU GOLLOP YOUR BEER WITH ZEST?

If so! You are unanimously elected a Member of

Ye Ancient Order of

Froth Blowers

REGD.

Life Membership 5/- with all the privileges of the proposed club house, including the use of corkscrews, sawdust, note and other paper, silver cuff-links, etc.

THIS ANCIENT GUILD (Circa 1924) exists to foster the noble Art and gentle and healthy Pastime of FROTH BLOWING amongst Gentlemen-of-Leisure and Ex-Soldiers. After payment of Subscription you will be *Permitted* to Blow Froth off your own beer, other members' beer, and occasionally off non-members' beer, provided that they are not looking or are of a peaceful disposition.

Special Privilege :— IMMUNITY FROM ARREST.

The Metropolitan Police have been requested not to arrest, annoy, or apprehend any member under or over the influence of Froth, should the said member be wearing the A.O.F.B. cuff links at the time of the debauch.

"DRINKS ROUND"

If not wearing A.O.F.B. Links when challenged.

This book and contents are written and copyrighted by Bert Temple.

2

A. O. F. B.

'ALE FELLOW, WELL MET!

"STAMPA."

3

AOFB Handbook. (Friends of the Froth Blowers)

The result was a significant increase in the level of donations. It should be borne in mind that this was at a time of great depression, so it is all the more remarkable that the organisation attracted people from all walks of life and classes of society.

Sadly, with the death of both Sir Alfred and Bert, and the demise of the mouthpiece of the organisation, *The Sporting Times*, the order finally ceased on 8 December 1931. The accounts showed that all creditors and staff were paid in full, and the remaining funds were distributed between the Hackney Branch of the Invalid Children's Aid Association, the Foundling Hospital Site Appeal Fund, Lady Fripp's Children's Xmas Dinners Fund and Bisley School.

One charity originally set up by Sir Alfred is, at the time of writing, still in existence. The Ancient Order of Froth Blowers Girl Guides & Boy Scouts administers and runs the Heartsease Guide and Scout Hut at West Wickham.

Sadly records of members and the activities of Flintshire VATs do not appear to exist, but it is assumed that their remaining funds were distributed amongst local charities.

However, not everyone used the organisation for peaceful purposes. In 1982, Colonel 'Mad Mike' Hoare and forty-two fellow mercenaries entered the Seychelles with the purpose of overthrowing the socialist government. Their cover was that they were a club on a rugby and beer-drinking trip – The Ancient Order of Froth Blowers – but this cover was blown when weapons were found in their baggage.

If you want to learn more about the Froth Blowers for purely peaceful purposes, or perhaps to join the friends of the AOFB, go to www.frothblowers.co.uk.

Z

ZULU WARS AND SOCIETY WEDDINGS

Many readers will have watched the film *Zulu* at what seems like every Christmas since it was made in 1964, and admired the performance of a young Michael Caine in his first starring role as the upper-crust Lieutenant Gonville Bromhead VC.

The Bromheads, with a long military pedigree, originated from Thurlby Hall in Lincolnshire. Members of the family served with distinction in campaigns from the American War of Independence to the Battle of Waterloo. The family has a number of connections with Flintshire gentry families, particularly that of the family of Rhual, on the outskirts of Mold. One, Basil Philips – later commanding officer of the 5th Battalion (Flintshire) RWF – was, like Gonville Bromhead, an officer in the 24th Regiment of Foot at the time of the Zulu War. However, it is not believed he actually served in South Africa during the various engagements.

Colonel Charles James Bromhead, brother of Gonville, also fought in the Zulu War, and in 1901 we find him living at Plas Draw, near Ruthin. His contacts with the family of Rhual were obviously maintained, as we find him and his son, Major Richard Bromhead, attending the wedding of Commander Heaton of Plas Heaton, Henllan, with Gwenllian Margaret Philips, the only child of Lieutenant Colonel Basil Philips. As was the normal practice for society weddings, every detail was reported in the local newspaper, including who attended and a list of presents along with the donor. Colonel and Mrs Bromhead gave the couple a silver bread dish, and Major Bromhead's somewhat strange wedding gift was a Dunhill pipe!

This was not the end of the link with Flintshire as, on 12 December 1928, Major Bromhead attended a wedding at St Mary's church, Mold. The service, conducted by the Archbishop of Wales was for the marriage of Violet Hope Wynne-Eyton of Leeswood Hall and Alan John Fairbairn. The link with Rhual was maintained at this wedding as one of the attendants, aged 5, was the grandson of Lieutenant Colonel Philips – who went on to become Major Basil Heaton.

ZEEBRUGGE, LIVERPOOL FERRIES AND THE MOLD MARINE

During the First World War the port of Zeebrugge, in Belgium, was used by the Imperial German Navy, and U-boats using the harbour as a base posed a particular threat to Allied shipping. In an attempt to block the harbour, a decision was taken to sink ships across the entrance, which, even at the planning stage, was recognised as being a high risk strategy for the seamen and marines involved.

On 23 April 1918, an attack was led by an old cruiser, HMS *Vindictive*, three old cruisers for use as block ships, two commandeered Mersey ferries and two old submarines packed with explosives. The latter were intended to be used to blow up a viaduct connecting the German garrison on a small island to the mainland.

The two Mersey ferries, *Daffodil* and *Iris II*, built by Robert Stephenson & Co. of Newcastle-upon-Tyne, carried a large assault force to engage the German garrison on the island. They were chosen due to their carrying capacity and shallow draft, enabling them to sail over the covering mine fields and to navigate the shallow waters close to the island.

As the vessels were double-hulled they were considered almost unsinkable, but when a shell burst through the deck of the *Iris II* it offered no protection to the fifty-six marines waiting to disembark. Forty-nine were killed outright, and the remainder were seriously injured. As part of Allied propaganda the raid was hailed as a success and eight Victoria Crosses were awarded, but it totally failed in its objective to close the port. A total of seventy-five ships and approximately 1,700 men took part in the raid, and heavy casualties were incurred – 227 dead and 356 wounded.

On board HMS *Vindictive* was a Mold-born Royal Marine, Walter Whitley of Ffynnonfa Cottage, Maes-y-Dre, who prior to joining the marines was employed as a furnace man at the Alyn Tinplate Works, Denbigh Road, Mold. The *Vindictive* was at the vanguard of the attack, so the seamen and marines on board and in the landing parties came under heavy fire. At some stage Walter Whitley was seriously wounded, and he was brought back to the United Kingdom where he sadly died at the Royal Naval Hospital, at Chatham, on 17 July 1918. His death was keenly felt in his home town, and there was even a special medal struck by the Urban District Council. The funeral, with full military honours, was also observed by the large crowds lining Mold's streets as his body was conveyed to the town cemetery. He was buried in the family grave, and amongst the names of other family members it has the following inscription:

Also in Loving Memory of
Pte Walter Whitley RMLI
Son of the above named
Who was wounded in the raid on Zeebrugge and Ostend
On the Belgian Coast April 23 1918
And died in the Naval Hospital at Chatham
July 17 1918 aged 22 years
He has given his life for his country's cause
May he rest in peace.

The Zeebrugge Hero
Well done, well done ye hero bold
England swells it to and fro
Love for your country you have shown
Left dismayed the Zeebrugge foe
Sleep on brave heart in perfect peace
Your task on earth is done
For Christ our king shall crown you with
The crown of life you've won
HMS *Vindictive*.

As we commemorate the centenary of the First World War, with its horrendous loss of life, it is fitting that this compendium of stories finishes with the last verse of a poem written by J. Evans Hughes, of Bromfield, Mold:

We all knew Walter Whitley,
The heroic one from Mold,
In the sands of time the story
Of Walter will be told;
Today in peace he resteth
On that eternal shore,
Where life's great storms and trials,
And battles are no more.

We will remember them.

Bibliography and Sources

GENERAL RECORDS

@nswers Centre, Mold Town Library.
Flintshire Record Office, Hawarden.

NEWSPAPERS

The main sources for entries are:

Chester Chronicle
Chester Observer
Flintshire Chronicle
The Leader
Liverpool Mercury
North Wales Chronicle
Wrexham Advertiser

Also used:

Country Quest (the magazine for Wales and the Border).
Daily News (Perth, WA, Tuesday, 8 January 1907 (Chief Inspector Conquest)).

BOOKS AND ARTICLES

Aldous, R., *The Lion and the Unicorn – Gladstone vs Disraeli* (London: Pimlico, 2007).
'An Echo of Zeebrugge', Mold Library.
Ball, S., and I. Holliday (eds), *Mass Conservatism: the Conservatives and the Public Since the 1880s* (Abingdon: Frank Cass Publishers, 2002).
Bingley, Revd W., *North Wales* (1814).
Birch, H.K., *The History of Policing in North Wales* (Pwllheli: Llygad Gwalch, 2008).

Brown, R.L., 'Sad, Mad or Bad: the Case of Evan Jenkins, Rector of Manafon', *Montgomeryshire Collections*, vol. 83, pp.177–88 (1995).

Carr, A.D., 'Some Seventeenth-century Remedies', *Journal of Flintshire Historical Society*, vol. 24 (1969).

Coleman, S.J., *Lore and Legend of Flintshire* (Isle of Man: Folklore Academy, 1956).

Davies, A.L., 'Luftwaffe over Mold', *Ystrad Alun: Journal of Mold & District Civic Society* (2000).

Davies, J., *A History of Wales* (London: Penguin Books, 1994).

Davies, J., *et al.* (eds), *The Welsh Academy Encyclopaedia of Wales* (Cardiff: University of Wales Press, 2008).

Davies, K., 'The Druid Coinage and the Greenfield Valley', *Journal of Flintshire Historical Society*, vol. 39 (2012).

Davies, W.K., 'Maritime Activity and the Flintshire Economy in 1891', *Journal of Flintshire Historical Society*, vol. 39 (2012).

Dickens Jnr, C., *Life of Charles Mathews – Volume 1* (London: Macmillan & Co., 1879).

Dodd, Q., *The Practice* (Wrexham: Bridge Books, 2003).

Ebbs, C., *Underground Clwyd – The Armchair Explorer's Guide* (Chester: Gordon Emery, 2000).

Formby, H., 'A History of Ysceifiog' (2007). (Article available in Mold Library @nswers Centre.)

Fraser, M., 'Indomitable Little Lady', *Country Quest* (1938).

Gladstone, P., *Portrait of a Family – The Gladstones 1839–1889* (Thos Lyster Ltd, 1989).

Griffiths, M., *The History of the River Dee* (Llanwrst: Gwas Carreg Gwalch, 2000).

Hague, D.B., *Lighthouses of Wales* (RCAHMW, 1994).

Hansford, N., 'Growing up in Wartime', *Ystrad Alun: Journal of Mold & District Civic Society* (2006).

Heaton, B.H.P., *A Short History of Rhual* (Shrewsbury, 1987).

Hole, C., *Traditions and Customs of Cheshire* (London: Williams & Norgate, 1937).

Holland, R., *Haunted Clwyd* (Llanwrst: Gwasg Carreg Gwalch, 1992).

Holland, R., *Supernatural Clwyd* (Llanwrst: Gwasg Carreg Gwalch, 1989).

Hubbard, E., *The Buildings of Wales – Clwyd* (London: Penguin Books, 1986).

Humphreys, R., 'French Jesuits Exiled in North Wales in the Late Nineteenth Century', *Journal of the Merioneth Historical and Record Society* (2012).

Illustrated Exhibitor: The Great Exhibition of the Industry of all Nations (London: 1851).

Jenkins, G.H., 'From Ysceifiog to Pennsylvania: The Rise of Thomas Wynne, Quaker Barber Surgeon', *Journal of Flintshire Historical Society*, vol. 28 (1978).

Jenner, L., *Liverpool to Loggerheads* (Cilcain, Flintshire: Alyn Books, 2009).

Jones, I.W., *Hitler's Celtic Echo* (Cambridge: Pegasus, 2006).

Jones, P., *Jonah Jones – An Artist's Life* (Bridgend: Seren Books, 2011).

Jones, R.E., *Arian: The Story of Money and Banking in Wales* (Swansea: Christopher Davies Ltd, 1978).

Jones, T.L., *Rioting in North-East Wales 1536–1918* (Wrexham: Bridge Books, 1997).
Jones, T.L., 'The Holywell Workhouse' (1995). (Article available in Mold Library @nswers Centre.)
Jones, T.L., *X-Site* (Rhyl: Gwasg Helygain, 2002).
Langdale, N., *The Story of the Home Guard – The Real Dad's Army* (London: Arrow Books, 1974).
Meese, C.E., *The Foresters' Hall, Bagillt* (Bagillt History Club, 1991).
Morgan, P. (ed.), *The Tempus History of Wales* (Stroud: Tempus Publishing, 2001).
O'Kane, M., and J. Morgan-Guy, *Biblical Art from Wales* (Sheffield: Phoenix Press, 2010).
Owen, E., *Old Stone Crosses* (London and Woodall: Bernard Quaritch, Oswestry and Wrexham: Minshall & Co., 1886).
Owen, T.M., *The Customs and Traditions of Wales* (Cardiff: University of Wales Press, 1991).
Pennant, T., *The History of the Parishes of Whiteford, and Holywell* (London: B&J White, 1796).
Perfect, V., *Flint Castle* (Cilcain: Alyn Books, 2012).
Phoenix, R. and A. Matthews, 'A History of Hope and Caergwrle', *Journal of Flintshire Historical Society*, vol. 39 (2006).
Pratt, D. and M. Grant, *Wings across the Border – Book 2* (Wrexham: Bridge Books, 2005).
Pritchard, T.W., *A History of the Old Parish of Hawarden* (Wrexham: Bridge Books, 2002).
Pritchard, T.W., *Mold Town and Country* (Wrexham: Bridge Books, 2012).
Pritchard, T.W., *St Winefride, Her Holy Well and the Jesuit Mission, c. 650–1930* (Wrexham: Bridge Books, 2009).
Pritchard, T.W., *The Making of Buckley and District* (Wrexham: Bridge Books, 2006).
Redhead, B. and S. Goodie, *The Summers of Shotton* (London: Hodder & Stoughton, 1987).
Richter, D., 'The Welsh Police, the Home Office, and the Welsh Tithe War of 1886–91', *Welsh History Review Cylchgrawn hanes Cymru*, vol. 12, No 1 (1984).
Roberts, D. (ed.), *A Clwyd Anthology* (Bridgend: Poetry Wales Press Ltd, 1995).
Shotton High School, 'Survey of Merchant Shipping with Special Reference to the River Dee'. (Article available in Mold Library @nswers Centre.)
Smith, G., *A Century of Shotton Steel (1896–1996)* (British Steel Strip Products, 1996).
St Mary's church, Cilcain, 'An Introduction to Visitors'.
Symons, A.J.A., *The Quest for Corvo* (London: Cassell, 1934).
'Talacre and the Viking Grave', *Llandudno, Colwyn Bay and District Field Club*, vol. 18, pp. 42–50 (1931, 1932, 1933).
Taylor, M.V., 'Roman Flintshire', *Journal of Flintshire Historical Society*, vol. 9 (1922).
Tennant, R., *A History of Holywell and Greenfield* (Wrexham: Bridge Books, 2007).
Tennant, R., *A History of Six Villages* (Holywell: Delyn Press, 2003).
Tennant, R., 'The Celtic Christian/Viking Myth Standing Stones in Older North Flintshire (including the mystery of Maen Achwyfan)' (2011). (Article available in Mold Library @nswers Centre.)

Timbrell, W.F.J., 'Altar Plate in the Church of St Mary, Hawarden', *Journal of Flintshire Historical Society*, vol. 6 (1917).

Timothy, J.A., *Old Flint* (Mold: Studio 365, 1980).

Tucker, N., 'Rebecca on the Prowl', *Country Quest*, vol. 7, No. 5 (October 1966).

Watson, N. (ed.), *A Village of Verse* (Bagillt: Bagillt Heritage Society, 2001).

Williams, D., 'The Druid Coinage and the Greenfield Valley', *Journal of Flintshire Historical Society*, vol. 39 (2012).

Williams, H., *They Lived In Flintshire, Volume 1: 1733–1946* (Wrexham: Hughes & Son, 1960).

Williams, J.G., 'Witchcraft in Seventeenth-Century Flintshire – Part One', *Journal of Flintshire Historical Society*, vol. 26 (1973–74).

Williams, J.G., 'Witchcraft in Seventeenth-Century Flintshire – Part Two', *Journal of the Flintshire Historical Society*, vol. 27 (1975–76).

Wynne-Eyton, C.E., 'Records and Reminiscences' (Unpublished).

CENSUS

1861

1891

1901

1971

WEBSITES

www.abergelefieldclub.co.uk

www.airhistory.org.uk

www.almanac.com

www.archiveshub.ac.uk/features/0704owen.html

www.aviation-safety.net/wikibase/wiki.php?id=153453

www.bbc.co.uk/religion/religions/mormon/history/josephsmith_1.shtml

www.bbc.co.uk/wales/northeast/guides/halloffame/historical/raymond_hughes.shtml

www.bbc.co.uk/wales/northeast/sites/flintshire/pages/mendelssohn.shtml

www.bbc.co.uk/wales/religion/sites/timeline/pages/religion_in_wales_12.shtml

www.british-civil-wars.co.uk/biog/bradshaw.htm

www.beunos.com

www.buckleyatwar.webs.com/thebuckleybomber.htm

www.caerwys-town.com

www.cardiff.ac.uk/insrv/libraries/scolar/special/salisbooks.html

www.coflein.gov.uk/en/site/35820/details/FFERM+HOUSE

www.deeside.com/deeside/garrison-sergeant-major-deeside-awarded-freedom-city-london

www.dralun.wordpress.com/tag/quakers/
www.earlytelevision.org
www.flightglobal.com
www.flintshirewarmemorials.com
www.fplkwales.org.uk/mari.html
www.forum.armyairforces.com/RAF-Sealand-Deeside-Flintshire-North-Wales-UK-m190
www.fourposterbeds-carved.co.uk/history/history-2htm
www.frothblowers.co.uk
www.genuki.org.uk/big/wal/FLN/Cilcain/index.html
www.grosvenorestate.com
www.historyofparliamentonline.org
www.historytoday.com/christian-allen/atom-spy-klaus-fuchs-jailed
www.historytoday.com/paul-martin/verminclub-1948–51
www.holywell.wikia.com/wiki/Greenfield_Valley_Heritage_Park
www.imagingthebible.llgc.org.uk
www.jorvik-viking-centre.co.uk/the-vikings/35-
www.kathleenandmay.co.uk/history.html
www.heraldica.org/topics/orders/garterlist.htm
www.leaderlive.co.uk/news/120005/international-focus-on-roman-discovery-in
www.leeswoodcommunity.org.uk/history/pontblyddyn-church-history
www.lds.org
www.library.manchester.ac.uk/searchresourcesguidetospecialcollections/atoz/owens
www.wbo.llgc.org.uk/en/s-GRIF-MOS-1747.html
www.llgc.org.uk/index.php?id=inglebywatercolours
www.merkki.com
www.museumwales.ac.uk/en/1890//blog/mendelssohn1-in-north-wales
www.musicteachershelper.com
www.old-merseytimes.co.uk/ROYALCHARTER.html
www.pantasaph.org.uk/st_davids_church
www.paranormaldatabase.com/wales
www.thepeerage.com
www.poemhunter.com/francis-thompson/poems
www.poetry.eserver.org/light-brigade.html
www.primrose-league.leadhoster/history.html
www.pugin.com
www.rafburtonwood.org/sealand.html
www.roxburgheclub.org.uk
www.ryhdymwynvalleyhistory.co.uk
www.stbridget-dyserth.co.uk/hismich.html
www.shotwick.org.uk/tour.html
www.sites.google.com/site/stjohnspentrobin/history

www.songsandhymns.org/people/detail/felix-mendelssohn
www.thepeerage.com
www.terrorfliegerwarlog.co.uk
www.historytoday.com/paul-martin/vermin-club-1948–51
www.victorianweb.org/authors/hopkins/hopkins12.html
www.watchhuman.co./birthday-1/c-4544.html (Tompion-Mostyn Clock)
www.wbo.iigc.org.uk/en/s-MOST-MOS-1301.html
www.wellhopper.wordpress.com/category/county/flintshire
www.welshjournals.llgc.org.uk
www.en.wikepedia.org/wiki/Charles_Kingsley
www.en.wikepedia.org/wiki/George_Edmund_Street
www.en.wikipedia.org/wiki/HMS_Bellerophon_(1786)
www.en.wikipedia.org/wiki/Zeebrugge_Raid

Also from The History Press

WHEN DISASTER STRIKES

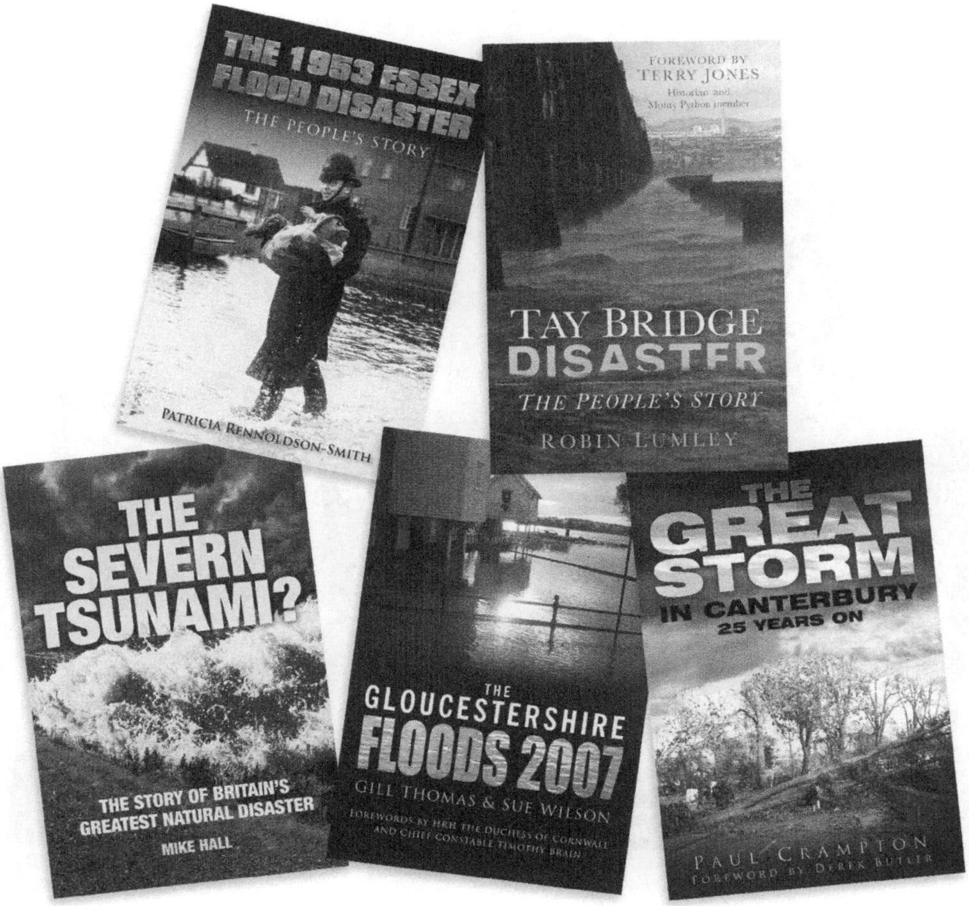

Find these titles and more at

www.thehistorypress.co.uk

The History Press

Lightning Source UK Ltd.
Milton Keynes UK
UKOW06f1544250315

248520UK00001B/5/P